AMERICA the BEAUTIFUL

WASHINGTON

By R. Conrad Stein

Consultants

David L. Nicandri, Director, Washington State Historical Society

Robert L. Hillerich, Ph.D., Bowling Green State University, Bowling Green, Ohio

CHILDRENS PRESS®

CHICAGO

A flower farm in Skagit County

Project Editor: Joan Downing
Associate Editor: Shari Joffe
Design Director: Margrit Fiddle
Typesetting: Graphic Connections, Inc.
Engraving: Liberty Photoengraving

Library of Congress Cataloging-in-Publication Data

Stein, R. Conrad.
    America the beautiful. Washington / by R. Conrad
Stein.
        p.   cm.
    Includes index.
    Summary: An introduction to the geography,
history, economy, people and interesting sites of the
Evergreen State.
        ISBN 0-516-00493-X
    1.   Washington (State)—Juvenile literature.
[1.   Washington (State)]   I.   Title.
F891.3.S74   1991   91-13509
979.7—dc20   CIP
                                                          AC

P+b

Mountain climbers on Mount Rainier

TABLE OF CONTENTS

Chapter 1
WELCOME
TO WASHINGTON

WELCOME TO WASHINGTON

Wagon trains rolling west some 150 years ago opened the land of present-day Washington to the American people. Settlers found this wilderness to be overwhelming in its beauty and its potential. Divided by the mighty Cascade Range, the region nourished junglelike forests west of the mountains, while treeless plains prevailed to the east. The settlers turned to logging and farming, and thrived on the generous land. The spread of railroads sparked the growth of lumbering, and as industry flourished, new towns sprang forth. In the twentieth century, industry took the form of aircraft manufacturing. Washington became the headquarters of the world's largest producer of heavy airplanes.

Despite its wealth of resources and scenic marvels, Washington long remained something of a mystery to most Americans. Only those who lived in the state were fully aware of its charms. Today, some people suggest that Washingtonians wanted to keep their homeland a secret, as if their secrecy would protect the gates of paradise. Nevertheless, the wonders of Washington eventually became known to the world. Now, tourists, job seekers, and students flock there each year. Washington has become one of America's fastest-growing states.

A few Washingtonians lament the flood of newcomers. Older residents may remember with pleasure a time when their cities were sleepy and their farmlands unmarred by superhighways and shopping malls. Still, Washingtonians welcome newcomers and acknowledge that their state will grow with change.

Chapter 2
THE LAND

THE LAND

*I saw from my home thousands of sunsets over Mt. Adams
and Mt. Rainier, their glaciers tinged with red or gold as if
some artist of Paul Bunyan proportions were using their ice
fields as his canvas.*
—William O. Douglas, *Of Men and Mountains*

GEOGRAPHY

Washington lies in the northwest corner of the lower forty-eight
states. Its location makes it the crown of the strikingly beautiful
region known as the Pacific Northwest. Washington is bordered
by Idaho on the east, Oregon on the south, the Pacific Ocean on
the west, and the Canadian province of British Columbia on the
north.

On a map, the state of Washington looks roughly rectangular in
shape, with a "bite" taken out of its northwest corner at the
Pacific Ocean. Below this watery nibble runs the long, narrow
Puget Sound. Cities along the banks of the island-studded Puget
Sound hold more than half of the state's residents.

Washington spreads over 68,139 square miles (176,480 square
kilometers) and ranks twentieth in size among the fifty states.
Olympia is Washington's capital; Seattle is its largest city.

THE COAST AND THE OLYMPIC PENINSULA

An eagle soaring over the length of Washington's seacoast
would fly 157 miles (253 kilometers) from the state's southern

San Juan Island in Puget Sound

border to its northern border. A hiker trekking the coastline, however, would be faced with a far longer journey. Including bays, capes, and the many islands in Puget Sound, Washington has more than 3,000 miles (4,828 kilometers) of coastline.

At the state's southern border with Oregon, the coastline yawns open to receive the waters of the mighty Columbia River. North of the Columbia River gap are Willapa Bay and Grays Harbor, two natural ports for oceangoing boats. This southwestern section of Washington, dominated by the Willapa Hills, is part of a topographical region known as the Coast Range. Farther north along the coast is the Strait of Juan de Fuca, which ships pass through to enter Puget Sound.

Between the Pacific Ocean to the west, the Strait of Juan de Fuca to the north, and Puget Sound to the east, sprawls a wilderness wonderland called the Olympic Peninsula. Rising up from the

The Olympic Peninsula, in northwestern Washington, includes huge areas of unspoiled wilderness.

Olympic Peninsula are the glacier-studded Olympic Mountains. The peninsula also contains dark forests, ferocious rivers, diamondlike lakes, and rugged hills free of roads or trails.

A FASCINATING VARIETY OF LAND FORMS

Within a single day's drive from the Washington coast lie lush forests, snow-covered mountains, endless miles of gently rolling farmland, and stark but beautiful deserts. Few other states contain within their boundaries so many radically different landscapes.

Mountains near the coast influence the climate farther inland and add to the state's crazy-quilt patchwork of land regions. Moist air sweeping in from the Pacific Ocean is deflected upward as it

The mighty Cascade Range divides eastern and western Washington.

encounters the mountains. As the ocean air rises, it loses moisture in the form of rainfall. Consequently, the western, or Pacific, side of the mountains receives far more rainfall than the eastern side.

The great Cascade Range, just west of the Puget Sound Lowland, is the primary shaper of Washington's climatic regions. East of these mountains, rainfall is much less abundant, and deserts prevail in some sections. In the Cascades stand Washington's tallest and most famous peaks: Mount Rainier, Mount Adams, and Mount St. Helens. On a clear day, Mount Rainier—the majestic symbol of the Northwest—can be seen from downtown Seattle, more than 60 miles (97 kilometers) away.

The part of the state that lies east of the Cascades, often called Washington's "Inland Empire," is made up of two regions. The Columbia Plateau, a dry but fertile basin, covers much of the

Arid badlands (left) and rolling, irrigated farmland (right) can be found in eastern Washington.

central and southeastern part of the state. Water brought by irrigation systems has allowed this area to support a $3-billion-a-year agricultural enterprise. The Columbia Mountains, an extension of the great Rocky Mountains, cover the northeastern corner of Washington.

RIVERS AND LAKES

The broad Columbia River is Washington's most important river. The Columbia begins far to the north in Canada and enters Washington near its northeastern corner. Twisting in a generally southerly direction through eastern and central Washington, it makes a sharp bend to the west at the town of Wallula. The mighty river then serves as the border between Washington and

The Yakima River flows through south-central Washington.

Oregon as it flows toward the Pacific Ocean. The Columbia winds some 700 miles (1,127 kilometers) through Washington and drains more than half the water that falls on the state.

The Snake, a branch of the Columbia, is Washington's second-largest river. Other major tributaries of the Columbia include the Colville, Pend Oreille, Sanpoil, and Spokane in the east; the Methow, Okanogan, and Yakima in the central part of the state; and the Cowlitz and Lewis rivers in the west. The Nisqually, Cedar, Nooksack, Skagit, Skykomish, and Stillaguamish are the most important rivers that flow into Puget Sound. On the west coast, the Soleduck, Hoh, Quinault, and Chehalis rivers empty directly into the Pacific Ocean.

Washington's many mountains combine with its river system to produce spectacular waterfalls. Among the state's most exciting

Abundant rainfall has produced lush rain forests on the Olympic Peninsula.

falls are the Cascade, Fairy, Palouse, Horseshoe, Klickitat, Nooksack, and White River.

About a thousand freshwater lakes dot the land of Washington. Major lakes on the Olympic Peninsula are Ozette, Crescent, and Quinault lakes. Long and narrow Lake Chelan, in the Cascade Mountain region, is the state's largest natural lake. Lake Washington, in Seattle's backyard, is a popular playground for city dwellers. Biggest of the state's lakes is Franklin D. Roosevelt, a long narrow body of water created by Grand Coulee Dam.

PLANTS AND ANIMALS

Forests, consisting mainly of pines and firs, cover almost half of the state. It is no wonder, then, that Washington's nickname is the

Lomatiums (left) and lupines (right) are among the many varieties of wildflowers that grow in Washington.

Evergreen State. Throughout the state's history, lumbering has been an important industry. The largest trees grow in the rain forests along the western slope of the Olympic Mountains. Scientists define a rain forest as an area that receives at least 80 inches (203 centimeters) of rain a year. Parts of the Olympic Forest are pelted with 150 inches (381 centimeters) of rain annually. Trees in the Olympic region are moss-covered because of frequent rains, and stand so close together that their tangle of branches blocks out the sun even on the brightest days.

Washington's wide variety of climatic regions breeds a rich array of plant life. Mountain slopes blaze with wildflowers such as Indian paintbrush, goldenrod, black-eyed Susans, and lupines. Rhododendron cover the hills on the Coast Range and at the base of the Cascades.

Wild animals thrive in the Evergreen State. Mountain lions roam the foothills of the Olympic Mountains. Rare mountain goats live in the higher elevations. Bears, elk, and deer inhabit the forests. Mink, muskrats, and beavers scurry about the marshlands. Bird life includes grouse, western larks, goldfinches, and wild ducks and geese. In inland lakes and streams swim rainbow trout, whitefish, sturgeon, and steelhead trout. Washington residents often gather on riverbanks to watch salmon—some weighing 50 pounds (23 kilograms) or more—struggle against rapids while obeying an instinct to lay their eggs in the fresh water upstream.

The Washington seashore nurtures its own special world of wildlife. Over the beaches and cliffs fly such shorebirds as oystercatchers, western gulls, and cormorants. Seals and sea lions frolic on the slippery rocks below the cliffs. Plying the offshore waters are killer whales that swim in packs.

CLIMATE

The great Cascade Mountains, Washington's towering "backbone," prevent warm Pacific air from flowing inland. As a result, western Washington has a far milder climate than the eastern portion of the state. For example, Seattle, west of the Cascades, averages about 41 degrees Fahrenheit (5 degrees Celsius) during January. However, the January temperature in Spokane, far east of the Cascades, averages a chilly 21 degrees Fahrenheit (minus 6 degrees Celsius). Summers tend to be moderate in the west, while the east can experience torrid temperatures. The thermometer once climbed to 118 degrees Fahrenheit (48 degrees Celsius) near Ice Harbor Dam in southeastern Washington.

Total precipitation (which includes both rain and melted snow)

The Skykomish River in winter

is influenced by the coastal mountains and the Cascades. While abundant rain urges moss-covered rain forests to sprout up from the western slope of the Olympics, larger areas of land east of the Cascades receive only 6 inches (15 centimeters) of rain a year. Most of the state's snow piles up on the lofty peaks of the Cascades. The heaviest winter-season snowfall ever reported in the United States came in 1970-71, when blizzards buried the slopes of Mount Rainier with 1,027 inches (2,609 centimeters) of snow.

Chapter 3
THE PEOPLE

THE PEOPLE

We are transients on these hills and shores, and the waters are not ours to spend. Here we mark some proof that urban man can live and work in a beautiful land without destroying beauty.
—Seattle civic leader James R. Ellis, speaking in 1966

POPULATION AND POPULATION DISTRIBUTION

Washington is one of the nation's fastest-growing states. The 1980 census counted 4,132,204 people living in the state, more than twice the census figure of forty years earlier. The 1980s were another growth decade, with an estimated 16.8 percent increase in the state's population. Seattle and its suburbs alone were estimated to have gained nearly 400,000 residents from 1980 to 1990.

Washington's population is booming, largely because of an influx of modern-day "settlers" from other states. Three main factors attract the new immigrants: Washington's agricultural- and industry-based economy promises jobs, the state's most populous region enjoys a mild climate, and Washington is considered one of the most beautiful of the fifty states.

Washington's population is unevenly distributed. Most of the state's people prefer the milder climate near the ocean. About three of every four Washingtonians live west of the Cascades, leaving the state's vast Inland Empire underpopulated by comparison. Two-fifths of the people live in the Seattle area.

Washingtonians of Scandinavian descent celebrate their cultural heritage at the annual Skandia Midsommar Fest in Poulsbo.

About 75 percent of Washingtonians reside in cities and towns, with the largest cities clustered in the Puget Sound area. Washington's Inland Empire, east of the Cascades, has three major urban centers: Spokane, Yakima, and the Tri-Cities—Richland, Pasco, and Kennewick. In order of population, Washington's largest cities are Seattle, Spokane, Tacoma, Bellevue, and Everett.

WHO ARE THE WASHINGTONIANS?

Washington's early settlers were farmers and loggers, most of whom were of German or Scandinavian heritage and came from the midwestern states. Washington's location on the Pacific Ocean, which made it a gateway to the Orient, also attracted Asian immigrants. People of Chinese and Japanese heritage have lived in Washington since the earliest days of non-Indian settlement. African Americans and people of Hispanic origin arrived in large numbers during and after World War II. The waves of immigration left modern Washington with a population that is 97 percent white, 2 percent black, and the remaining 1 percent divided among Asian, Hispanic, and Native American peoples.

Native Americans (American Indians) were Washington's first inhabitants. Today, about 105,000 Indians live in the state. Thirty-five thousand of these people reside on one of Washington's twenty-six Indian reservations.

The majority of Washingtonians are members of Protestant denominations. Leading Protestant groups include members of the Church of Jesus Christ of Latter-day Saints (also known as Mormons), Methodists, Lutherans, and Presbyterians. Roman Catholics make up the state's largest single religious group, claiming nearly half a million members. About twenty thousand Washingtonians are Jewish.

LIFESTYLES AND POLITICS

Washingtonians live with nature at their front door. Even in the crowded cities along Puget Sound, a family is just a short drive from a lonely forest trail or a rugged mountain peak. It is estimated that one in every five Washington households owns a boat. Fishing or camping equipment hangs in nearly every Washington garage. Slade Gorton, a United States senator from Washington, symbolizes the people's zest for outdoor adventures. Gorton once took his entire family on a journey across the width of the United States—on bicycles.

Because Washingtonians so love nature, many fear the state's unchecked population growth. Housing complexes, shopping centers, and schools are spreading across the land at an astonishing pace. In metropolitan areas, land that twenty years ago was farmland now sprouts endless rows of single-family houses. New highways, supermarkets, and parking lots are advancing relentlessly into Washington's wilderness areas.

Seattle in particular has experienced runaway growth. Seemingly overnight, it changed from a quiet, unhurried town to a bustling major city. Its wildest period of development occurred during the 1980s, when a forest of high-rise buildings sprang up, permanently altering Seattle's skyline. After the seventy-six-story Columbia Seafirst Building was completed in 1985, Seattle residents cried out, "Enough!" Concerned citizens backed laws regulating further growth and restricting future high-rises to a forty-story limit. A leading figure in the Seattle preservation movement was journalist Emmett Watson of the *Seattle Times*. Said Watson, "My message is basically, don't turn the town over to developers."

In the 1930s, the state's voters began developing what would be a longtime preference for the Democratic party. Two powerful Democrats—Warren Magnuson and Henry Jackson—represented the state in Congress for a combined total of eighty-seven years. In recent years, however, voters have pursued a more independent course, and no party has claimed a lock on them.

Washington voters often surprise the experts. In 1976, they elected Dixy Lee Ray governor. A professor of zoology at the University of Washington, Ray had never before served in a high government office. Many voters agreed with her strong support for the building of nuclear power plants in Washington. Seattle, a city whose population is only 10 percent black, elected an African American, Norman Rice, as its mayor in 1989. Said Rice of his ever-expanding city, "Seattle is . . . ready to get to its next level of maturity. People coming here now are secure in what they want out of life."

Chapter 4
THE BEGINNINGS

THE BEGINNINGS

There was a time when our people covered the whole
land, as the waves of a wind-ruffled sea covers its floor.
—Chief Seathl, for whom Seattle was named,
speaking in 1854

THE FIRST WASHINGTONIANS

Long before recorded history began, men and women migrated
from Asia to North America. It is widely believed that these
ancient peoples crossed a land bridge that once existed in the
Bering Sea. Hundreds of years later, their descendants pushed into
the region now known as the Pacific Northwest.

The first Washingtonians found the land alive with exotic
animals, such as mastodons, mammoths, and giant beavers. In the
1970s, at a farm outside the town of Sequim, archaeologists found
dramatic evidence of an ancient hunt when they uncovered
mastodon tusks and a crude weapon made of animal bones.
Radiocarbon tests determined that the weapon and the tusks were
between twelve thousand and fourteen thousand years old.
Excavations also revealed the remains of ten-thousand-year-old
pit houses in the southeastern part of the state. A typical pit house
was circular, dug about 3 feet (1 meter) into the ground, and
topped by a structure made from poles.

Along the Olympic Peninsula lived groups of fishermen who

Petroglyphs (left) and such objects as this wooden carving of a whale fin (above) are among the artifacts left behind by some of Washington's earliest-known inhabitants.

ventured into the Pacific in huge, well-crafted, wooden canoes to hunt whales. On cliffsides, they drew vivid rock paintings that are still visible today. Many of these drawings, called pictographs, are of whales. Pregnant whales are depicted as large whales drawn over the figures of smaller whales. Ancient petroglyphs— drawings carved into rock—are found throughout the state.

The state's best preserved archaeological site is at Ozette, near Neah Bay on the Olympic Peninsula. Some five hundred years ago, a village at Ozette was buried by a sudden mud slide. The disastrous wave of mud destroyed the people's houses, but preserved many of their contents. Prior to the mud slide, the Ozette site had been occupied for more than fifteen hundred years. Among the ruins, archaeologists have found such remarkable items as planks covered with whale-figure carvings, and a wooden carving of a whale fin inlaid with hundreds of sea-otter teeth.

A nineteenth-century photograph of a Makah woman drying fish

LIFE DURING THE CONTACT PERIOD

About seventy different tribal groups lived in what is now
Washington during the "contact period," when the Indians first
encountered white explorers. Because the land was so radically
divided by the Cascade Range, two distinct Indian cultures had
developed.

Native Americans west of the Cascades enjoyed a lifestyle of
plenty in a land rich in natural resources. Their rivers teemed
with fish, and forests nurtured by generous rainfall provided deer,
elk, and other game. Major groups residing west of the Cascades
included the Chinook, Clallam, Clatsop, Makah, Nooksack, and
Puyallup.

On special occasions, such as a royal marriage, tribal leaders in the coastal region demonstrated their wealth by hosting lavish parties called potlatches. The word *potlatch* comes from the Chinook language and means "to give." During such a party, the host chief was expected to show his generosity by offering nearly all his possessions to his guests. The great celebration usually left the host chief impoverished, but the coastal people believed that sharing their goods was more rewarding than accumulating them.

In sharp contrast to those who lived on the bountiful coast, those living in the harsher land east of the Cascades sometimes experienced famine. Villages in the inland region were clustered along riverbanks, where the inhabitants fished for salmon. So important were the salmon that the inland people regarded them as gifts from the gods. Each year, the first migrating salmon was caught and taken to the village. There, amid religious singing and dancing, the fish was prepared and eaten. Its bones were then carefully placed back into the river in the hope that the gods would assure the village a successful salmon harvest.

The people of inland Washington hunted deer, elk, moose, and smaller animals. They also gathered wild berries and roots. The roots of the camas plant, which when boiled taste like sweet potatoes, were especially prized. Because wild game was sometimes scarce in inland Washington, the people moved often. They lived in easily constructed dugouts—rough shelters dug into the side of hills or trenches and covered with mats of grass. Among the groups living east of the Cascades were the Cayuse, Colville, Nez Perce, Spokane, and Yakima.

For the most part, the inland and coastal peoples had little contact with one another. However, along the Columbia River, a lively trade took place. The Chinook—who lent their name to a species of salmon—were perhaps the greatest traders in the Pacific Northwest. Though the tribes of the Washington region spoke a dizzying variety of languages, most used Chinook words when bartering goods. Often, dozens of tribal groups gathered at The Dalles, a fishing ground on the Oregon side of the Columbia River, to trade, dance, tell stories, and run races.

The inland and the coastal peoples worshipped a single, all-powerful creator and a host of lesser gods and spirits. Often the great creator was depicted in religious drawings as a coyote. Each village had at least one shaman, who served as spiritual leader as well as medicine man. A skilled shaman could acquire power rivaling that of the village chief. Belief in the existence of a thunderbird so large that its wings blotted out the sun was common among coastal people. It was said that the thunderbird hunted whales by diving into the sea and carrying them off to its mountain lair.

THE EXPLORERS

From the time Christopher Columbus touched upon the shores of the New World, European sea captains sought a waterway that would allow them to sail west through the North American continent and reach the rich markets in the Orient. European mariners called the waterway the "Northwest Passage." For three centuries, seafarers tried, without success, to discover this fabled sea channel. Though the Northwest Passage did not exist, its quest hastened the exploration of North America's shores.

In 1592, Greek sea captain Apostolos Valerianos, using the Spanish name Juan de Fuca, claimed he sailed along Washington's shores and discovered the Northwest Passage. Historians doubt many details of Juan de Fuca's voyage, but the strait that runs from the Pacific to Puget Sound still bears his name. During the late 1700s, British sea captain James Cook and another Englishman, John Meares, explored the Pacific Coast in search of the Northwest Passage. Meares saw and named Mount Olympus in 1788.

Rhode Island-born sea captain Robert Gray was the first American to arrive in the region. While leading a trading expedition in 1792, Gray noticed an enormous gap in the rocky coastline. He edged his ship toward the gap, and after fighting a treacherous current, sailed into a broad river never before seen by whites. He called the river *Columbia*, naming it after his ship.

That same year, the search for a Northwest Passage led Great Britain to send George Vancouver to the Puget Sound area. For two years, Vancouver remained in the Pacific Northwest, carefully mapping the coast and giving names to outstanding land and sea features: Puget Sound, named after Vancouver's lieutenant, Peter Puget; Mount Baker, named after a crewman; Mount Rainier, named after Vancouver's friend; and Whidbey Island, named after crewman Joseph Whidbey.

The most adventurous expedition to the Pacific Northwest began in 1804, after American president Thomas Jefferson sent former army officers Meriwether Lewis and William Clark on a cross-continental mission of discovery. Leaving the western outpost of St. Louis on the Mississippi River, Lewis and Clark trekked more than 1,700 miles (2,736 kilometers) over unknown and unexplored land. After a grueling eighteen-month journey, the party followed the Columbia River Basin and reached its destination—the glimmering Pacific Ocean. The Lewis and Clark expedition provided information that would strengthen the United States's future claim to the explored regions.

Fort Vancouver (right) was founded in 1825 by John McLoughlin (above).

A CLASH OF NATIONS

By the early 1800s, interest in the Northwest Passage faded, but merchant nations still coveted the Washington region because it was rich in beavers and other fur-bearing animals. At various times, Russia, Great Britain, Spain, and the United States laid claim to what would become present-day Washington and Oregon. Eventually Spain and Russia withdrew their claims, leaving the young United States and its former colonial master, Great Britain, to compete for supremacy in the region.

The land the two nations coveted was known as the Oregon Country. The word *Oregon* came from an Indian name for the Columbia River. The Oregon Country was huge, much of it was unexplored, and it had no set boundaries. Generally, Old Oregon started at California, stretched north to Alaska, and spread from the Rocky Mountains west to the Pacific Coast.

Scotsman John McLoughlin emerged as Old Oregon's most dynamic leader. As head of the British-owned Hudson's Bay fur-trading company, McLoughlin built Fort Vancouver along the Columbia River in 1825. The city of Vancouver now rises at the site of the old fort. Under McLoughlin's direction, Fort Vancouver became an island of European civilization in the midst of the northwestern wilderness. A few years after its founding, the fort protected a hospital and a scattering of homes where as many as five hundred people lived. Always a visionary, McLoughlin fostered the development of agriculture in the Oregon Country by encouraging people to save and plant the seeds left over from their meals. It is said that the tasty apples for which Washington is now famous were first planted at Fort Vancouver.

At the height of the fur-trading era, the Hudson's Bay Company operated posts in Colville, Okanogan, and Walla Walla, and ran farms near the present-day towns of Chehalis and Steilacoom. However, the expansion of the fur trade brought disaster to the Native Americans in the Oregon Country. Lured by white men's goods, such as fishhooks and rifles, some Indians gave up their time-honored occupations as independent hunters to become hired trappers for the fur-trading companies. Worse yet, the white traders brought to the area such diseases as smallpox, diphtheria, and measles, against which the Indians had no immunities.

In the eastern United States, political warfare brewed over the ownership of the Oregon Country. Sweeping through the United States was the spirit of "manifest destiny," an almost religious belief that it was God's will for the American nation to expand from the Atlantic to the Pacific. In 1844, James Polk ran for president under the campaign slogan "Fifty-Four Forty or Fight!"

Polk and his backers demanded that the British give up their claim to all the Oregon land south of latitude 54° 40', a boundary that lies near present-day Alaska. The British, realizing they were outnumbered in the Northwest, eventually reached a compromise with the United States. In 1846, Britain agreed to a treaty recognizing as American territory all the land south of the 49th parallel—Washington's present boundary with Canada. The Oregon Country was now officially part of the United States.

THE MISSIONARIES

The most famous missionary group to come to the Oregon Country was led by Americans Marcus and Narcissa Whitman. In 1836, the Whitmans arrived in Oregon after an exhausting trip that had begun in New York. Narcissa Whitman and Eliza Spalding, another missionary wife in the party, were the first white women to complete the overland journey across the continent. Whitman kept a journal of the trek over the Rocky Mountains. In one entry, she expressed, "We had no sooner gained one mountain when another more steep and dreadful was upon us." The Whitmans established a mission among the Cayuse Indians near present-day Walla Walla.

The missionaries in Old Oregon had mixed success. They found the Native American people willing to listen to Bible stories, but unwilling to renounce their ancient beliefs in spirits and lesser gods. The Indians, in turn, regarded the missionaries with curiosity and fear. They learned that wherever American missionaries set up a church, American settlers were sure to follow and encroach on Indian land. Moreover, the missionaries were able to help many whites recover from diphtheria and measles—diseases brought to the region by the whites—but failed

Above: Narcissa Whitman
Left: Whitman Mission
National Historic Site

to cure the Indians. Neither group realized that the whites had greater immunity to these diseases and therefore were more likely to recover.

The measles epidemic that swept inland Washington in 1847 was particularly deadly. The Cayuse who lived near Walla Walla became convinced that the white missionaries were poisoning them so that American settlers could claim their land. On a strangely silent morning, November 29, 1847, Cayuse warriors attacked the mission run by Marcus and Narcissa Whitman, killing them and twelve others.

The massacre triggered the Cayuse War. American settlers living in the Willamette Valley of present-day Oregon organized a makeshift army and marched east. The outnumbered Cayuse hid in the forest, where many died from hunger and frigid temperatures. To save the tribe, five Cayuse men surrendered. These five men were given a hasty trial and hanged.

The Cayuse War failed to diminish the hopes of immigrants coming to the Oregon Country. Over the next three decades, waves of Americans arrived to settle in Old Oregon, the land they believed would fulfill their dreams.

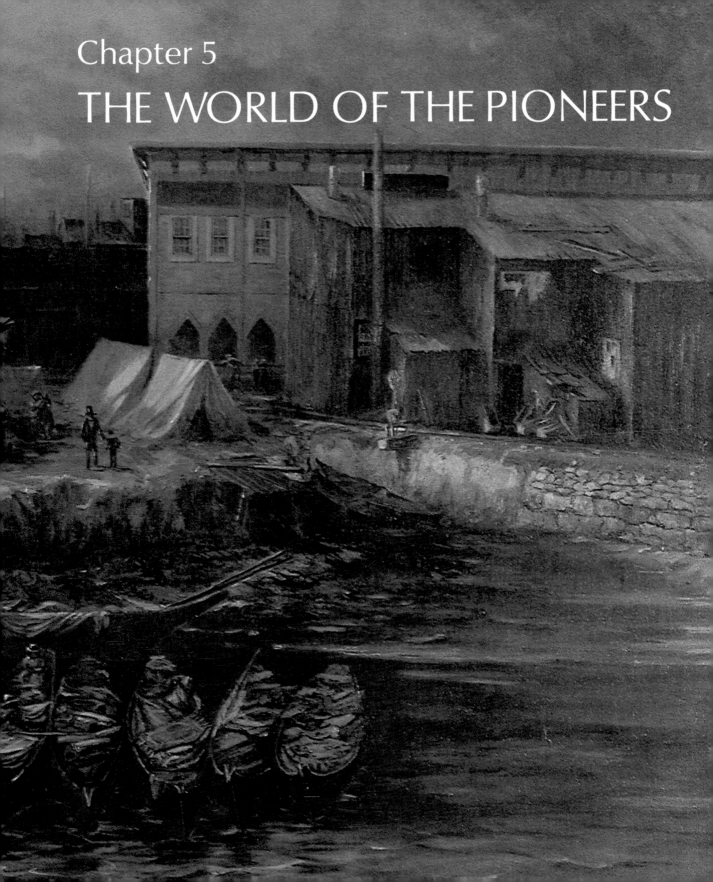

Chapter 5
THE WORLD OF THE PIONEERS

THE WORLD OF THE PIONEERS

Come as soon as you can. We have found a valley that will support a thousand families.
—David Denny, one of the founders of Seattle, in an 1851 letter to his brother

OREGON FEVER

"Eastward I go only by force. But westward I go free. . . . This is the prevailing tendency of my countrymen. I must walk to Oregon," said Henry David Thoreau, the writer and naturalist from Massachusetts. During the 1840s and 1850s, hordes of American farmers caught the same "Oregon fever" that exhilarated Thoreau, and began the long trek to the Northwest.

Responding to the interest in the Pacific region, Congress created the Oregon Territory in 1848. The Oregon Territory was a sprawling land mass made up of the present-day states of Washington, Oregon, Idaho, and parts of Montana and Wyoming. Thousands of people decided to try to settle in the virgin area.

The promised land of Oregon Territory was 1,500 miles (2,414 kilometers) away from the nearest town on the western frontier. To reach the Oregon wilderness, a family had to journey along the Oregon Trail. The Oregon Trail has been romanticized in hundreds of stories and songs. In truth, the trip over the

An engraving showing westward-bound pioneers fording the Snake River

Oregon Trail was exhausting and filled with dangers. Even so, the people came. Between 1840 and 1860, an estimated three hundred thousand Americans took the Oregon Trail to California or to the Oregon Territory.

To prepare for the long journey, families formed wagon trains at frontier outposts such as Independence or St. Joseph, Missouri. Sometimes the wagon trains were led by Kit Carson, Joe Meek, or other famous figures of the American West. Members of the train began their long march with the command, "Wagons, ho!" Then—with cows mooing, dogs barking, and wagon wheels squealing—the travelers pushed west. The trail led across the grasslands of the Midwest and twisted up the rugged Rocky Mountains. At Fort Hall, in present-day Idaho, it branched, and Oregon-bound immigrants separated from those bound for California.

During the course of their journey, the travelers forded rushing rivers and took their wagons over tortuous mountain passes. Making 14 miles (23 kilometers) a day was considered good progress. Though the people lived in fear of Indian attacks, actual fighting between immigrants and Native Americans was rare. The settlers' deadliest enemy was the disease cholera, which spread quickly from one wagon-train member to another. Those stricken with cholera experienced intense stomach pains and uncontrollable vomiting. Sufferers usually died after twenty-four pain-wracked hours. During the pioneer years, more than thirty thousand immigrants died from various causes and were buried along the Oregon Trail.

Most travelers reached their destination, however, filling Oregon's Willamette Valley with farms. It was several years before the overflow of pioneers began gazing north of the Columbia toward the wilderness land in Washington.

THE NEW TERRITORY

The official 1850 census counted about thirteen thousand Americans in Oregon Territory, but only about a thousand lived north of the Columbia River in present-day Washington. Those early Washingtonians felt woefully isolated from their government. Their territorial capital, in what is today Salem, Oregon, lay across the unbridged Columbia and over many miles of rugged roads. Settlers who lived north of the Columbia held two meetings to draw up plans establishing a new territory. One meeting took place in 1851 at the tiny village of Cowlitz Landing; the other convened in Monticello (present-day Longview) a year later. At the meetings, drafts for the first division of Oregon Territory were agreed upon and sent to Washington, D.C. The proposed new territory was to be called Columbia, but lawmakers in the nation's capital changed the name to Washington to honor the first president of the United States.

On March 2, 1853, President Millard Fillmore signed the bill creating the Washington Territory. At first, the new territory included parts of present-day Idaho and Montana. Congress later adjusted the boundaries, and ten years after its birth, Washington Territory had the same borders as the present-day state.

SETTLING THE WILDERNESS

The promise of free land acted as a magnet, drawing masses of settlers to the Pacific Northwest. In 1850, Congress passed the Donation Land Act, which gave away as much as 640 acres (259 hectares) of land in the Oregon Territory to any farm family agreeing to work the claim for at least four years. This land-giveaway program was one of the most generous in American history. The measure had its faults, however. By law, blacks were forbidden to claim land, as were unmarried women and foreigners. Not even Native Americans—who were considered foreigners despite having lived on the land for thousands of years—were entitled to land grants.

Because the land-giveaway program attracted hordes of people, towns began to develop in the Washington Territory. The first wilderness towns were logging seaports clustered in the Puget Sound region. The village that became Seattle was founded in 1851 by a group headed by the Denny family of Illinois. They eventually named the town after Chief Seathl, a Duwamish Indian who had been friendly to them. When building their first shipping dock, the residents of early Seattle set out in a boat and used Mrs. Denny's clothesline—weighed down by a horseshoe—to

An early painting of the Seattle waterfront

determine the depths of offshore waters. Tacoma was born in
1852, when a Swedish immigrant named Nichalas de Lin built a
water-driven sawmill there. It was said the local Indians were so
fascinated watching de Lin's machine slice through huge logs that
millworkers had to push their way through crowds to get at the
controls. Olympia, first settled in 1846, was also a shipping port
for logging firms, but the town turned quickly to the business of
government. Throughout the territorial period, Olympia served as
Washington's capital.

Centralia, south of Puget Sound, was founded by a former slave
named George Washington. When he was a baby, Washington was
purchased by James and Hannah Cochran, who educated him and
later granted him freedom. He traveled with the Cochrans to the

Port Townsend, by nineteenth-century artist Harriet Foster Beecher

Washington Territory, where the Cochrans were given a generous land grant. Free land was denied to Washington because of his skin color. But through logging and farming, Washington earned enough money to buy the Cochrans' claim at $1.25 an acre. Years later, he established the city of Centerville (now called Centralia) and sold housing lots to families. Washington donated the land to build a church, a park, and a cemetery. Centerville became one of the most prosperous towns on the Washington frontier.

Not so sterling a community was Port Townsend, on the northern tip of Puget Sound. The federal government moved its customshouse from Olympia to Port Townsend in 1853, and all ships entering Puget Sound had to stop and register there. The stop gave sailors the opportunity to drink and gamble with the local loggers. Port Townsend was famed and feared for the brawls that broke out in waterfront taverns.

Arrival of the Nez Perce Indians at Walla Walla Treaty May 1855

Arrival of the Nez Perce Indians to The Wallawalla Treaty May the 1855

The arrival of the Nez Perce at the 1855 Walla Walla conference

While new settlers poured into the Puget Sound region, development occurred at a much slower pace in eastern Washington. A lack of rainfall and the presence of hostile Indians discouraged farmers from settling what is today Washington's Inland Empire.

TREATIES AND WARS

Walla Walla. May 29, 1855. For the white men present, the scene must have been awe-inspiring. Some six thousand Indians representing various tribes in eastern Washington had gathered in a wilderness clearing to discuss a treaty. Several famous chiefs were there: Weyatenatemany of the Cayuse, Lawyer of the Nez Perce, Wenapsnoot of the Umatilla, Kamiakin of the Yakima, and

Nez Perce chief Lawyer (left) and Walla Walla chief Peo-Peo-Mox-Mox (right) were among the Indian leaders who attended the 1855 Walla Walla conference.

Peo-Peo-Mox-Mox of the Walla Walla. Facing the great council of tribes was a delegation of sixty white men headed by Isaac Stevens, the first territorial governor of Washington.

Isaac Stevens was a brilliant man who had finished first in his class at West Point. But he had political aspirations and was driven by ambition. Also, his sensitivity toward the Indians and their way of life was slight. One way to impress his superiors in Washington, D.C., was to deliver treaties that opened up new lands to white settlers while pushing the Indians aside. There were rumors of gold in northeastern Washington along the Colville River, and Stevens wanted to finish negotiating with the Indians before they became aware of the potential worth of the land they would be ceding.

At the Walla Walla conference, Stevens gave the Indians little choice. The white authorities had set aside special areas, called reservations, where the Indian population was assigned to live. They could either accept the reservations picked out for them, or go to war and risk losing their land altogether. The various tribes disagreed over what action to take. After nearly three weeks of debate, the tribal leaders signed the document. Once more, Isaac Stevens had secured a lopsided treaty that fostered white expansion at the expense of the Indians.

The treaty and others like it fueled Indian frustration and triggered the Indian wars that raged in the Washington Territory between 1855 and 1858. The situation was aggravated as white settlers poured into Washington in search of gold.

The most violent fighting of the Indian wars took place in eastern Washington. In May 1858, a group of one thousand Indians routed an army led by Colonel Edward Steptoe. In response to Steptoe's defeat, Colonel George Wright led a huge force on a mission determined to punish the Indians. Wright burned Indian houses, hanged leaders, and even shot his enemies' horses. The colonel's brutal tactics worked, and the Indians returned to their reservations.

For nearly twenty years, a grim peace settled on the Washington frontier. Then, in the 1870s, whites in Oregon and Washington began settling on land belonging to the Nez Perce. Headed by Chief Joseph, the Nez Perce fought back. The Indians had little success against the United States Army, but Chief Joseph led his tribe on a brilliant escape that frustrated the cavalry units assigned to pursue him. When he was finally forced to surrender, Chief Joseph gave a moving speech: "It is cold and we have no blankets. The little children are freezing to death. . . . My heart is sick and sad. From where the sun now stands I will fight no more forever."

Chief Joseph (third from right), shown here with his family, tried to lead several hundred Nez Perce to safety in Canada after the United States government forced them to leave their traditional homeland in Washington and Oregon.

THE RAILROADS

Isolation plagued the settlers of Washington. The overland trip to the eastern states took four months. Letters from home arrived long after they were written. Washingtonians took heart in 1869, when the first transcontinental railroad was completed. It linked Sacramento, California, with the East Coast. A few years later, the Northern Pacific railroad company planned a second continental route that would run from the East to Puget Sound. The news electrified frontier Washington.

Railroads meant riches, and suddenly people in every sleepy Washington hamlet hoped the Northern Pacific would run down their main street. Seattle competed with Tacoma to become the

The inauguration of Washington's first state governor, Elisha P. Ferry, was held in Olympia on November 11, 1889.

terminus (end) of the Northern Pacific line. Business leaders in Seattle offered the railroad 3,000 acres (1,214 hectares) of free land if their city were chosen as the terminus. Eventually, the Northern Pacific chose Tacoma, because it had a better ocean port. Business leaders in Tacoma—which at the time was larger than neighboring Seattle—moved nearly every building in their business district to accommodate the railroad's right-of-way.

The Northern Pacific Railroad was completed in 1883. Towns along its route suddenly stirred with business activity. In Spokane, a local newspaper reported, "New dwellings, new stores, and new manufacturing establishments are springing up like magic, and the end is not yet." Towns such as Wallula and Pasco, which existed only to serve the railroad, sprouted up beside the tracks. Yakima community leaders were outraged when the Northern Pacific chose to run its tracks 4 miles (6 kilometers) north of the village. But when tempers cooled, the shrewd residents simply jacked up their houses, put them on wheels, and rolled them near the tracks. The move took two weeks. En route, Yakima's major hotel stopped at a new location each night, and still opened its doors to take in lodgers.

Railroad fever struck once again when tycoon James Hill began construction of the Great Northern—a rail line connecting Puget Sound with St. Paul, Minnesota. The city of Everett was chosen to be a major terminal of the Great Northern, and so many speculators came to buy land that local stores sold out all their beds. The incoming businessmen were forced to sleep in coffins provided by Everett's undertaker. The Great Northern, completed in 1893, whisked passengers from St. Paul, Minnesota, to Seattle in just three days.

STATEHOOD

The ever-increasing population brought by the railroads made the Washington Territory eligible for statehood. Delegates met at Olympia to draw up a state constitution. The territory's voters approved the constitution by a four-to-one margin, and the document was sent to the nation's capital. On November 11, 1889, President Benjamin Harrison signed the law making Washington the forty-second state to enter the American Union.

Elisha P. Ferry, a Seattle banker and two-term territorial governor, was elected as Washington's first state governor. The new government acted quickly to promote higher education. Just three years after Washington became a state, the legislature created Washington State College at Pullman and established teacher's colleges at Cheney, Ellensburg, and Bellingham.

Largely because of the railroads, 357,232 people were living in Washington by 1890, an increase of 375 percent in just ten years. Clearly, the Evergreen State was on the move.

Chapter 6
TWENTIETH-CENTURY WASHINGTON

TWENTIETH-CENTURY WASHINGTON

People from the north, east, south, and west, take my advice, go and make your home in Wonderful Washington. The climate is pleasant. There are splendid opportunities for both capital and labor.
—From an early twentieth-century brochure entitled "Wonderful Washington"

THE INLAND EMPIRE

During the pioneer era, most newcomers to Washington headed directly to the Puget Sound region. The vast inland area east of the Cascades remained underpopulated because pioneers believed it was too dry for farming. Instead of farms, it primarily supported cattle and sheep ranching. Yet eastern Washington had fertile soil and enjoyed about three hundred sunny days a year. In order to support productive farming, the region needed only water.

The first large-scale irrigation project took place in the town of Sunnyside, which lies along the Yakima River. Sunnyside was settled by a religious community whose members tried, unsuccessfully, to channel the waters of the Yakima onto their farms. In 1905, however, the federal government took over the project, with successful results. Given a regular supply of water, farmers in the rich Yakima Valley near Sunnyside grew abundant crops of asparagus, tomatoes, and sugar beets. Following the Sunnyside example, many other communities abandoned ranching, devised irrigation systems, and raised crops.

Eastern Washington became a world-famous producer of apples (above) after irrigation was brought to the region in the early 1900s (left).

In the early 1900s, an apple craze swept eastern Washington. Orchards, nurtured by irrigated water, sprouted up near the cities of Okanogan, Wenatchee, and Yakima. Washington became the nation's largest apple producer. But the abundant crops of juicy Washington apples flooded the market, causing the prices to drop. Many eastern Washington orchard owners went bankrupt.

Wheat emerged as the king of crops in eastern Washington. Whitman County, in the southeastern part of the state, grew the most valuable wheat crop of any county in the nation in 1910. Wheat farming gave rise to a rural milling industry. Eastern Washington towns such as Dayton, Pomeroy, Ritzville, and Waitsburg all developed as small milling communities.

THE GROWTH OF THE CITIES

On a summer day in 1897, the steamship *Portland* eased into the Seattle harbor carrying $800,000 worth of gold from the Klondike

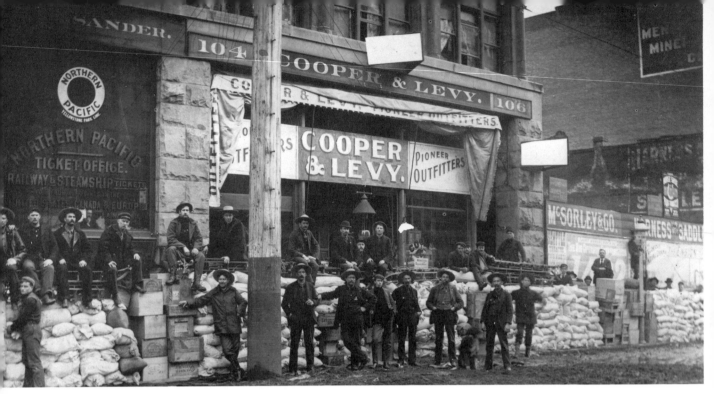

Seattle was the main supply center for the Klondike gold rushers.

region of Canada's Yukon Territory, just across the border from Alaska. A newspaper writer named Erastus Brainerd heard about the rich cargo and wrote a sensational story claiming that a ship laden with "a ton of gold" had docked at Seattle. The story triggered the great Klondike gold rush. Thousands of hopeful miners raced to Seattle to book passage for Alaska and the Klondike. Seattle itself attracted newcomers as well, as the city became the main supply center for the gold rushers. The growth of the lumbering, shipping, and fishing industries also drew people to the area. Between 1900 and 1910, Seattle's population nearly tripled.

Other coastal towns experienced steady, though less spectacular, growth. Aberdeen and Hoquiam expanded as fishing ports. The United States Navy built a shipyard in Bremerton in 1891. One of the state's busiest sawmill towns was Everett, which by 1900 was home to ten shingle mills, eight sawmills, and a huge pulp mill.

At the turn of the century, many small cities in Washington were devoted to one primary business activity. Canners in Puyallup packed berries and fruits. Anacortes was a fish-canning center. Coal mining dominated Black Diamond, Carbonado, and Wilkeson. Bellevue was the home port of a tiny whaling fleet. Burlington, Chehalis, and Mount Vernon were marketing towns that served nearby farmers. Kirkland was founded on the dream of English millionaire Peter Kirk, who planned to build a huge steel mill on the town site. The mill never materialized, but Kirkland still became a thriving community.

The state's fastest-growing city was Spokane. In 1880, Spokane was a fledgling village of 350 people. By 1910, its population topped 100,000, making it Washington's second-largest city. Spokane's growth was spurred by the railroads and by industry that sprouted up to serve lead and silver mines in nearby Idaho.

INDUSTRY, LABOR, AND THE PROGRESSIVE MOVEMENT

''The Truth Is Good Enough,'' rang the theme of the Alaska-Yukon-Pacific Exposition, which opened in Seattle in 1909. The exposition was designed to show the world the amazing progress Washington had made in just twenty years of statehood. More than 3.7 million people attended the fair, and President William Howard Taft delivered a major speech there.

Despite Washington's achievements, masses of people suffered poverty and had little voice in state government. Farmers were at the mercy of the railroads, which charged unreasonably high freight rates to ship produce to market. Loggers earned just two dollars a day and were forced to sleep in crowded, insect-infested bunkhouses. Women in Washington—as in the rest of the nation—were denied the vote.

To redress their grievances, farmers and workers turned to a new political organization called the Populist party. The Populists won an important victory in 1896, when their candidate, John R. Rogers, was elected governor. Rogers, a former newspaper writer from Puyallup, signed laws that regulated railroad freight rates, improved working conditions in mines, and created the state's first Bureau of Labor.

In 1910, Washington became the fifth American state to extend voting rights to women. One of the leaders of the state's woman suffrage movement was May Arkwright Hutton, who lived in Spokane. As a young woman, Hutton ran a boardinghouse catering to railroad workers. She managed to save a few dollars, and made a modest investment in an Idaho silver mine. The mine struck a fabulously rich vein of silver, making Hutton a millionaire. In Spokane, Hutton became active in state politics and was a powerful force in securing the vote for Washington women.

Out of the Populist party and the woman suffrage drive grew a new political force called the Progressive Movement. Leaders of the movement hoped to place the power of government directly into the hands of the voters. The Progressives concentrated on passing four reform measures: the direct primary, which allowed voters to choose their own candidates for office; the referendum, which permitted voters to approve or turn down laws passed by the state legislature; the initiative, a process giving voters the right to initiate (begin) the writing of a new law; and the recall, a method allowing voters to remove a government official. By 1912, all four measures had been passed into law.

During World War I, the sprawling Fort Lewis army base was built near Tacoma. Wartime demands kept the lumber camps and the shipyards working at a furious pace. But labor unrest struck Washington at the war's end.

Many Washingtonians, including these members of a communal colony established by Socialists, began pressing for social reforms in the early 1900s.

Long active in the state was an organization called the Industrial Workers of the World (IWW), which sought to unite working people into a powerful industrial army. In February 1919, Seattle's shipyard workers, seeking better pay, walked off their jobs. The IWW called on all union members to strike in sympathy with the shipyard workers. A strange hush overcame Seattle as the nation's first successful general strike paralyzed the city. The Seattle strike was settled quickly, but eight months later, violence flared up at Centralia. American Legion members held a parade there to celebrate the nation's first Armistice Day. As the legionnaires passed the local IWW organizing hall, shots rang out and four marchers were killed. No one knew who fired first. The celebration turned into a riot, and a mob beat and lynched one IWW member.

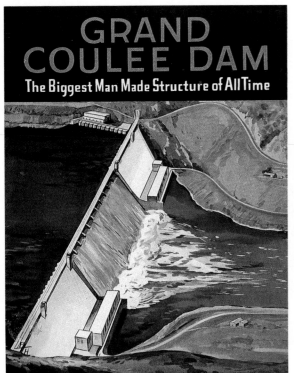

The construction of Grand Coulee Dam (left), which created many jobs, was part of the federal government's attempt to alleviate the hardships brought on by the Great Depression (right).

THE DEPRESSION AND WORLD WAR II

Washington's industrial growth staggered when the Great Depression gripped the nation in the 1930s. During the height of the depression, one-third of the state's industrial workers were jobless. Particularly hard hit was the lumbering industry; 80 percent of the mills were forced to close. Loggers who kept their jobs suffered pay cuts, driving down their wages to $3 per day.

In the 1932 election, the vast majority of Washingtonians cast their votes for two Democrats: Franklin D. Roosevelt for president, and Clarence D. Martin for governor. Martin, a wheat farmer from Cheney, was the first Washington governor to be born in the state.

During the depression years, the federal government launched an ambitious dam-building program in Washington. In 1933, work began on Bonneville Dam, whose locks were built on the Columbia River near the town of Stevenson. Grand Coulee Dam, which was begun in 1936, was called the "biggest construction job on earth." The structure was designed to provide electric power and to bring irrigation waters to central Washington. Constructing Grand Coulee Dam gave seven thousand jobs to depression-wracked Washington workers.

The Japanese bombs that rained down on Pearl Harbor on December 7, 1941, shocked the nation out of the Great Depression and into World War II. In Washington, the once-idle shipyards in Seattle, Tacoma, Bremerton, and Vancouver began to buzz with activity. Some forty thousand workers assembled ships in Seattle; yards in Bremerton employed thirty thousand. A new industry — aluminum — bloomed during the war years, as plants were constructed in Vancouver and Longview. Workers, including great numbers of blacks, streamed in from other states to claim jobs. During the 1940s, the state's black population increased fourfold.

One carefully guarded wartime project was undertaken at the village of Hanford, near Richland, where a small army of workers gathered and lived in hastily built wooden dormitories. Before long, Hanford held fifty thousand people, making it the fifth-largest city in the state. Secrecy was so great at Hanford that only a few of the workers knew that plants there were making plutonium, a key ingredient for the atomic bomb.

Washington's most celebrated contribution to World War II victory came from the Seattle-based Boeing Company. Boeing, a pioneer aircraft firm, began producing B-17 heavy bombers in the late 1930s. Boeing plants assembled thirteen thousand B-17s to

meet wartime demands. Boeing's second-generation bomber, the
B-29, dropped bombs on Japanese cities late in the war years.
A B-29 built by Boeing dropped an atomic bomb on Hiroshima in
1945, ending the war but bringing the world into the frightening
age of nuclear warfare.

While World War II brought jobs and money to Washington, it
also unleashed long-held racial prejudices. For generations, whites
in the Pacific Coast states had resented their Asian neighbors. In
Washington, laws had been passed restricting Asians from buying
land and settling in certain communities. When the war broke
out, many people of Japanese ancestry who lived on the West
Coast were accused of being spies, even though no evidence of
their disloyalty existed.

Early in 1942, President Franklin D. Roosevelt signed a law that
forcibly removed all people of Japanese heritage from California,
Oregon, and Washington, and placed them in "relocation camps"
in the Rocky Mountains and in the midwestern states. They were
forced to remain in the camps throughout the war. One of the few
politicians to speak against this brutal treatment of Japanese
Americans was Tacoma mayor Henry P. Cain. Washington voters
later elected Cain to the United States Senate.

THE POSTWAR PERIOD

Suburbia! After World War II, the growth of Washington's
suburbs seemed almost magical. Land that once supported farms
was suddenly covered by look-alike houses, grids of streets, and
shopping centers. The Puget Sound region led the state in
suburban development. From Everett to Tacoma, a long, narrow
megalopolis began to form. Suburbs such as Lynwood and Federal
Way emerged from what had been tiny farm communities.

This Washington family was among the thousands of Japanese Americans who, during World War II, were ordered by the federal government to leave their homes on the West Coast and move to inland "relocation camps."

Bellevue, a suburb of Seattle, was Washington's fastest-growing town in the postwar years. Before the war, Bellevue was a village sitting on the shores of Lake Washington at Seattle's back door. A remarkable floating bridge built during the 1940s spanned Lake Washington at Mercer Island and eased the commuting time between Bellevue and Seattle. The onetime village soon acquired its own industries and a glass-and-steel downtown.

In the 1950s, Richland was called the "Atomic City" because of the nearby Hanford Project's contribution to the atomic bomb. Following the war, the reactor at Hanford produced plutonium for even more powerful nuclear weapons. Soon, people living near Richland and the neighboring cities of Kennewick and Pasco noticed some frightening occurrences. Children of the area suffered from swollen necks caused by inflamed thyroid glands.

An unusual number of babies were born with underdeveloped lungs and heart problems. Many years passed before it became known that deadly radiation leaking from the "Atomic City" was poisoning the countryside.

After the war, Boeing engineers shifted from constructing piston-driven planes to building jet-powered craft. In 1952, the company test-flew the giant B-52, a jet-driven heavy bomber that remained in use in the 1990s. Boeing also began marketing the 707, a passenger jet that became the workhorse for almost every commercial airline in the world.

MODERN WASHINGTON

Brass bands and fireworks marked the opening of Century 21, the world's fair held in Seattle in 1962. The fair, designed to promote tourism in Washington, ran six months and drew 9.5 million visitors. Legacies of the fair are many present-day Seattle landmarks, including the Space Needle, the futuristic monorail, the Opera House, the Coliseum, and the Pacific Science Center.

By the early 1960s, Boeing employed fifty-eight thousand Washingtonians, more people than the company had employed at the height of World War II. Boeing's spectacular growth caused many political leaders to fear that the state would become overdependent on a single industry. Indeed, any slowdown at Boeing could trigger a statewide recession in Washington. Yet, for the most part, Boeing's 707s and other planes sold faster than the workers could assemble them.

The late 1960s was a time of strife in the nation and in the Evergreen State. As the war in Vietnam escalated, police clashed with demonstrators in Seattle's streets. Native Americans and white sports enthusiasts fought over fishing rights granted in

Several famous Seattle landmarks, including the Pacific Science Center (left) and the Space Needle (right), were built for Century 21, the world's fair held in Seattle in 1962.

century-old Indian treaties. Black student organizations grew more militant on college campuses.

The 1960s was also a time when Washingtonians took a hard and often painful look at their polluted rivers and lakes and their forests laid waste by logging. Environmental issues began to dominate the political battlegrounds of Washington. The state enjoyed great success cleaning up its waterways. Lake Washington, long a playground for Seattle residents, had become so polluted that it was declared unsafe for swimming. Sewage runoff was the main source of the pollution. To rescue the lake, voters in Seattle, Bellevue, and other communities approved an expensive plan to build sewage disposal plants. In eastern Washington, the Spokane River had become polluted, largely

This series of photographs shows Mount St. Helens just before (left), during (right), and after (opposite page, left) the 1980 eruption; and some of the destruction left in the wake of the eruption (opposite page, right).

because mines had dumped wastes into the river for decades. The river was cleaned up in time for Expo '74, Spokane's world's fair. A safe and beautiful environment was the theme of the exposition.

The power of nature awed Washingtonians and the world when Mount St. Helens erupted on May 18, 1980. Earlier, in March, the 10,000-foot (3,048-meter) volcano had begun to rumble and give off steam. Earthquakes rattled the region. Finally, the volcano top exploded with the terrifying force of several atomic bombs. In eastern Washington, a cloud of smoke and debris billowing out of the volcano turned day into night and covered nearby towns with a blanket of ash. Sixty people living near Mount St. Helens were killed.

In the 1980s and 1990s, logging practices spurred heated political debates. Environmentalists attacked the industry's policy of "clear-cutting"—felling nearly every tree in a region. Logging companies argued that clear-cutting was cost effective, and any other method of harvesting trees would force them to lay off workers. A particularly bitter struggle was waged over the cutting

of "old-growth" forests, those rare woodlands more than six hundred years old. Old-growth trees produce prized furniture because their wood is fine-grained and free of knots. In 1990, the federal government banned old-growth logging because the northern spotted owl, a vanishing species, lives only among the ancient trees. Environmentalists hailed the ban, but it cost thousands of jobs in Washington and Oregon.

In the early 1990s, Seattle gained nationwide attention for its effectiveness at waste reduction, an enormous task confronting many major cities. About 80 percent of Seattleites now participate in a curbside recycling program. This and many other efforts at waste control have underscored Washington's reputation of environmental concern.

Washingtonians look upon environmental problems as challenges they will surely meet and overcome. Through great effort, they have cleaned up their surroundings and now live in one of the healthiest and most beautiful of the American states. Certainly the newcomers flocking to the Evergreen State are discovering what Washingtonians have long known to be true: few places are more friendly or more livable than the state of Washington.

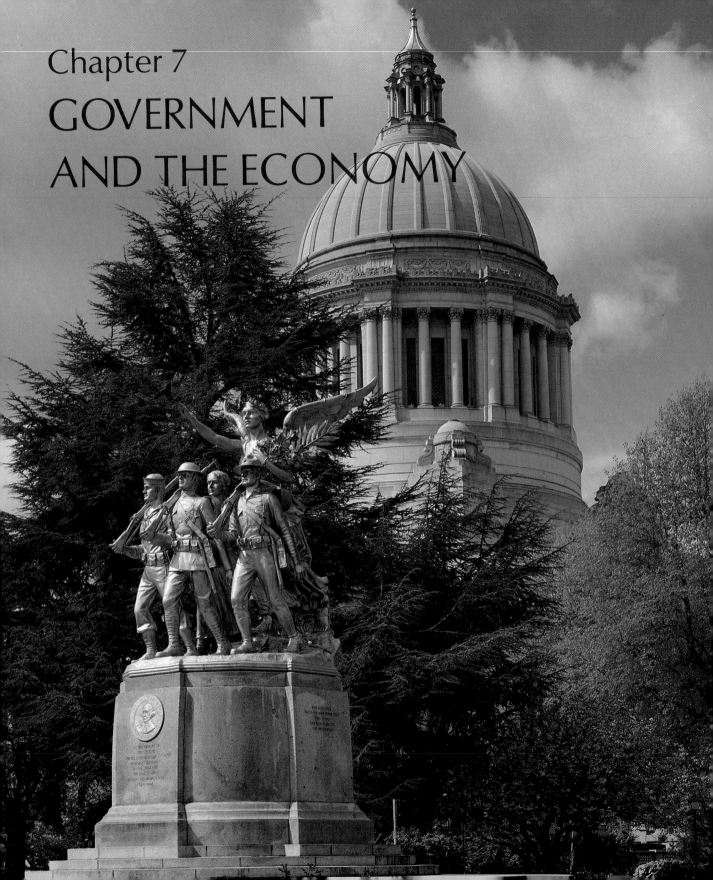

Chapter 7
GOVERNMENT AND THE ECONOMY

GOVERNMENT AND THE ECONOMY

GOVERNMENT

Washington is governed by its original constitution, which was written in 1889. Over the years, the constitution has been amended (changed) more than seventy-five times. The constitution divides state government into three branches or departments: the executive department, which carries out laws; the legislative department, which creates new laws and rescinds old ones; and the judicial department, which interprets laws and tries court cases.

The executive department is headed by the governor, who is elected to a four-year term. The governor may run for an unlimited number of additional terms. The constitution gives the governor broad powers, including the ability to call out the state militia in times of emergency. Other major elected officers include the lieutenant governor, auditor, attorney general, treasurer, and commissioner of public lands.

The legislative department consists of two bodies: a forty-nine-member senate and a ninety-eight-member house of representatives. Senators are elected to four-year terms; members of the house serve two years. New laws, called bills, are drawn up by the legislature and sent to the governor. When the governor signs a bill, it becomes a law. If the governor refuses to sign (vetoes) a bill, the legislature can override the veto by repassing the measure with a two-thirds vote of both houses.

The judicial department consists of the court system. The supreme court, made up of nine justices, is the highest court in the state. Lowest in the judicial system are municipal courts and district courts. Yet these courts hear nearly 90 percent of the cases argued in the state. In addition to trying criminal cases, the court system hears conflicts ranging from disagreements between huge corporations to squabbles among neighbors.

The cost of running state government is staggering. During the 1980s, the average annual budget topped $8 billion. Washingtonians pay the cost of government through a state sales tax and through special taxes on such items as gasoline, alcohol, and tobacco.

Local governments are administered by Washington's 39 counties and 266 incorporated cities and towns. A provision in the state constitution grants ''home rule'' to any city with a population greater than twenty thousand. This means that city voters may choose their own form of local government. Local governments perform duties such as maintaining a township police force.

EDUCATION

Financing the public school system is the most costly item on the state budget. In the 1980s, Washington taxpayers spent approximately $3,800 per year to educate each student. By law, children between the ages of eight and fifteen must attend school. The state has about 545,000 elementary students, 255,000 secondary students, and 38,000 teachers.

Higher education in Washington centers around its twenty-one degree-granting institutions. Serving nearly 35,000 students, the state-supported University of Washington at Seattle is the largest

Left: The campus of the University of Washington at Seattle
Right: Wheat being harvested on Whidbey Island

university. Other state-supported colleges include Washington
State University at Pullman, Western Washington University in
Bellingham, Central Washington University in Ellensburg, Eastern
Washington University in Cheney, and Evergreen State College
near Olympia. Major privately supported colleges are Gonzaga
University in Spokane, Seattle Pacific University and Seattle
University in Seattle, the University of Puget Sound in Tacoma,
and Whitman College in Walla Walla.

AGRICULTURE

Washington has about thirty-eight thousand farms that average
430 acres (174 hectares) in size. Wheat is the state's leading crop.
Washington is also a major producer of hops, hay, potatoes,
barley, sugar beets, and asparagus. Dairy farms are common in the

Washington, which produces a variety of fruits and vegetables (left), is the nation's leading grower of apples (right).

western part of the state, while cattle and sheep are raised on ranches east of the Cascades.

Washington is the nation's leading grower of apples. The state is famous for its Red Delicious and Golden Delicious varieties of apples. Other fruit grown in the state includes cherries, apricots, grapes, berries, and pears. Most Washington fruit is grown on irrigated fields in the central part of the state.

The cultivation of flower bulbs is a major enterprise. Tulip, daffodil, and iris bulbs grown in Washington are later planted in flower gardens throughout the nation. Washington greenhouses also raise such popular houseplants as azaleas, Easter lilies, and poinsettias.

Washington's flower farms, many of which are located in the Skagit Valley, explode into a riot of color every spring.

NATURAL RESOURCES

Washington's vast forests have long been its most valuable natural resource. In the 1980s, the timber industry employed some sixty thousand Washingtonians and earned $8 billion a year. Douglas firs and ponderosa pines are the main types of trees growing east of the Cascade Mountains; western hemlocks predominate in the rainier west. It is estimated that Washington has one-fifth of the nation's supply of Douglas firs. Sitka spruces, western red cedars, western larches, lodgepole pines, alders, aspens, cottonwoods, and maples are among the other kinds of trees that grow in Washington.

Commercial fishing (left) and lumbering (right) are two industries that
utilize Washington's abundant natural resources.

Washington is the only West Coast state with a significant
supply of coal. Most of the state's coal mines are found in Lewis
County in the southwest. Other minerals taken from the state
include lead, zinc, limestone, sand and gravel, clay, silver, and
gold.

Commercial fishing is a $90-million-a-year business in
Washington. Chinook and sockeye salmon are the prized catches,
but fully two hundred species of edible fish and shellfish swim off
the state's coast. Pacific cod, ocean perch, flounder, oysters, sole,
crabs, rockfish, herring, and tuna are seafoods harvested in
Washington.

MANUFACTURING AND SERVICE INDUSTRIES

Manufacturing is a $12.5 billion-a-year business and employs
some three hundred thousand Washington workers. Shipyards in

Boeing 747 jumbo jets are assembled at the huge Boeing plant in Everett.

Bremerton, Seattle, and Tacoma make Washington a major shipbuilder. Food processing, which includes canning and flour milling, is an important business. Nearly thirty-five thousand Washington men and women work in lumber mills and wood-product firms. Computer manufacturing and other high-tech industries are enjoying steady growth.

Aircraft and space products lead the state's manufacturing enterprises. The Boeing Company, headquartered in Seattle, employs nearly one hundred thousand Washingtonians. Major Boeing plants stand in Renton and Everett. The Everett factory, which rises ten stories and covers more than 60 acres (24 hectares), is the largest enclosed space on the planet. At Everett, workers assemble the wide-body 747-400, the latest of Boeing's jumbo passenger jets. In 1990, United Airlines placed a $22-billion order with Boeing, the largest contract ever awarded to an airplane manufacturer.

Bonneville Dam is one of several dams in Washington that were built to generate hydroelectric power and provide irrigation.

Service industries such as wholesale and retail trade, medicine, banking, and tourism are the state's largest source of jobs. Tourist-related businesses are the fourth-largest employer in the state. Every year, tourists spend more than $3 billion enjoying the sights and activities Washington offers.

WATER CONTROL AND POWER

The vast network of dams that harness Washington's rivers also make it the leading state in generating hydroelectric power. Along the Columbia River alone stand the Chief Joseph Dam at Bridgeport, McNary Dam near Kennewick, Rocky Reach Dam near Wenatchee, Bonneville Dam near Stevenson, John Day Dam near Goldendale, Wanapum Dam near Vantage, and the engineering marvel of the 1930s—Grand Coulee Dam. In addition to generating electricity, Washington's dams provide irrigation water for the normally dry eastern two-thirds of the state.

Nuclear power has had a spotty history in Washington. In the 1960s, a state agency called the Washington Public Power Supply System (WPPSS) decided to build five nuclear power stations at a cost of $6 billion. Accidents and squabbles among contractors drove up the estimated cost of the project to nearly $24 billion. Environmentalists objected to the nuclear facilities because of the possibility of a disastrous accident. In 1981, the WPPSS halted work on all but one nuclear generator. The project's failure triggered a financial crisis in Washington.

TRANSPORTATION AND COMMUNICATION

About 4,000 miles (6,437 kilometers) of railroad track cross Washington. Freight trains haul bulk loads such as coal. Passenger trains serve about thirteen cities. The Evergreen State has about 70,000 miles (112,651 kilometers) of paved roads. Always-busy Interstate 5 connects the Puget Sound communities. The Tacoma Narrows Bridge, which spans Puget Sound, is one of the world's longest suspension bridges. The Lake Washington Ship Canal, built in 1916, cuts across Seattle and links Lake Washington with Puget Sound. Washington's main shipping ports are Seattle, Tacoma, Anacortes, Bellingham, Longview, Kalama, and Vancouver. The state's largest airport, located between Seattle and Tacoma, is commonly called the Sea-Tac Airport.

Washington has about twenty-five daily newspapers. Leading dailies are the *Seattle Post-Intelligencer*, the *Seattle Times*, and the *SpokesmanReview* of Spokane. Some two hundred radio stations, twenty commercial television stations, and six educational television stations operate in the Evergreen State.

Chapter 8
ARTS AND RECREATION

ARTS AND RECREATION

ARTS AND CRAFTS

Washington's artistic heritage began with the Indians of the
Pacific Northwest, who produced beautiful crafts long before the
arrival of European settlers. The people of the coast, taking
advantage of the abundant forests, became master woodworkers.
From cedar or redwood they carved giant totem poles—perhaps
the best-known symbol of the Northwest Indians—as well as
elaborate chests, boxes, and masks. Erected in front of houses, the
totem poles contained animal symbols representing a family's
ancestry. People living along the Strait of Juan de Fuca used dog
hair to make warm and sturdy blankets and robes. Colorful straw
baskets woven by the inland peoples were so skillfully made that
they could hold water without leaking.

Even in the early frontier era, Washingtonians pursued the arts.
One pioneer artist was German-born Gustav Sohon, who, in the
1850s, often accompanied Territorial Governor Stevens on meetings
with Indian groups. Sohon drew the only surviving portraits of
prominent chiefs who lived in the Columbia River region.

Crafts flourished in pioneer times. Dutch settlers in the town of
Lynden were famous for their carefully hand-carved wooden
shoes. Finnish women living in Seattle did marvelous needlework
on tablecloths, blankets, and napkins.

Early in the twentieth century, Seattle residents organized the
Society of Seattle Artists, which sponsored the first exhibition of
Northwest art. Members of the society helped establish the

The Indians of the Columbia Plateau were known for their superb basketry (left), while those who lived along the coast were master woodcarvers whose creations included huge totem poles (above). These arts still flourish today.

Seattle Art Museum, which opened in 1933. Today, the Seattle Art Museum houses the state's largest collection of paintings and sculpture.

Washington's leading artist of the 1930s was Seattle resident Mark Tobey. Influenced by Asian art, Tobey developed a unique style that came to be called "white writing." Guy Anderson, Kenneth Callahan, and Morris Graves were other prominent Washington artists of the period. Using the town of Edmonds as a base, these painters launched a movement called the "Northwest School," which merged Asian painting techniques with the colors found in the forests and mountains of Washington and Oregon.

A daring group of artists live and work in Washington today. Sculptor Dale Chihuly fashions large and fascinating shell-like shapes out of glass. Another sculptor is George Tsutakawa, who has won national acclaim for his beautiful fountains. Jacob Lawrence renders historic scenes depicting such black liberators as

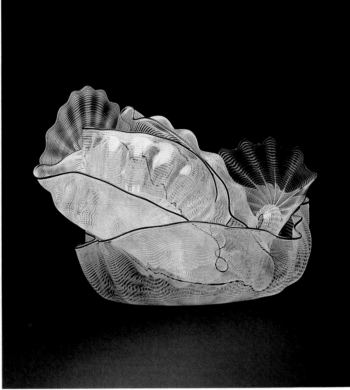

Works by Washington artists Mark Tobey (left) and Dale Chihuly (right)

Frederick Douglass and Harriet Tubman. Chari Markowitz is a painter and sculptor famed for her delightful animal heads.

LITERATURE

The earliest written accounts of Washington were the journals of explorers and adventurers. One such journal was written by New Englander Theodore Winthrop, who traveled the wilds of Washington, lived with the Indians, and described his experiences in a book called *The Canoe and the Saddle*. Fellow New Englander James G. Swan lived in Port Townsend and traveled the Puget Sound area in the 1850s. *Three Years Residence in the Washington Territory* was his account of his experiences.

Other than descriptive works, literature was slow to develop in the Evergreen State. The *Washington Magazine*, first published in

1889, was the state's earliest attempt to establish a literary journal. In the magazine's first issue, local historian Edmond Meany complained, "There is no time [in Washington] to devote to the production or the appreciation of a distinctive literature." Meany added, however, "Literature will be fostered by and by."

In 1912, Mary McCarthy was born in Seattle. Orphaned at a young age, she was sent to live in a stern household headed by her grandfather. McCarthy became a prominent novelist, renowned for her cutting wit. In her book *Memories of a Catholic Girlhood*, she describes this teenage experience: "I was not allowed to go out with boys, but one night the captain of the track team drove up to my house in his roadster and honked for me to join him. My grandfather flashed on the front porch lights and thundered at him to go away, and that was the end of my conquest."

William O. Douglas earned his place in American history by serving thirty-six years on the United States Supreme Court, a longer term than any other justice. Douglas was also a marvelous writer, producing books on such topics as world travel, politics, and the outdoors. He grew up on a farm near Yakima, where he acquired a love of hiking and mountain climbing. Though he lived in the nation's capital for many decades, he kept a house at Goose Prairie so he could be close to Mount Rainier. His most popular book was *Of Men and Mountains*, a powerful work describing his communion with the rugged Cascades.

Popular science-fiction writer Frank Herbert was born in Tacoma and as an adult had a home in Port Townsend. The novels of Herbert's *Dune* series carry readers to a fantastic, sandy-dry planet inhabited by a warrior people who ride about the vast deserts on gigantic worms. Another modern Washington writer is Carolyn Kizer of Seattle and Spokane, who won the 1985 Pulitzer Prize for poetry.

In recent years, writers from other states have moved to Washington. During the 1940s, poet Theodore Roethke came from Michigan to teach at the University of Washington. Roethke won both the Pulitzer Prize and the National Book Award. Ivan Doig, born in Montana, wrote *Winter Brothers: A Season at the Edge of America*. It retraces the journeys of James G. Swan, a Port Townsend resident who traveled through the Washington wilderness in the 1850s.

MUSIC AND THEATER

The untamed forests of Washington rang with music when settlement began. Heard often were the fishing songs of the Columbia River Indians, who chanted, "Oh-ah we-ah" when they caught a particularly fat salmon. One explorer called the fishing chants "a song too shrill for melody." French *voyageurs* sang special boat songs as they made their way along the rivers of the Northwest. The missionaries brought hymns such as "Rock of Ages," which the Indians learned quickly and sang beautifully. Singing in the Washington wilderness was sometimes accompanied by a fiddle or a banjo, but most often by no instruments at all. Settler Richard Covington was credited with bringing the first piano to Washington, when he shipped one to his Vancouver home in the 1840s.

During the pioneer era, German immigrants formed singing groups in their farm villages. Swedish, Norwegian, and Welsh singing societies also were started. Music halls opened in cities such as Tacoma, Olympia, and Seattle. African-American soprano Maggie Webb was a particularly popular performer who toured Washington's music halls.

Music and art in Washington received a tremendous boost in

Mountain climbing (left) and rafting (right) are among Washington's most popular outdoor activities.

1914, when Nellie Cornish opened the Cornish School of Arts (now Cornish College of the Arts) in Seattle. Cornish was a pianist with a lifelong interest in music, dance, and the fine arts. Talented musicians came from every part of the state to study at the Cornish School. The school also held classes in painting and sculpture, and some of the finest artists in the Northwest taught there.

Washington today offers music for everyone's taste—from classical to jazz to rock. The Seattle Symphony, organized in 1903, is the state's premier orchestra. After World War II, the Seattle Symphony was directed by renowned English conductor Sir Thomas Beecham.

The state's first known theater performance took place in 1853 when an actor who called himself "General" Jack Rag did a recitation in the dining room of Olympia's only hotel. Admission to Rag's performance was twenty-five cents. As more pioneers entered the state, theater groups performed in the cookhouses of lumber camps and in the storage rooms of sawmills.

By the turn of the century, theater was a thriving institution in Washington. Grand theater houses such as Squire's Opera House in Seattle, the Gaiety Theater in Walla Walla, and the Alpha Opera House in Tacoma drew enthusiastic audiences. The Auditorium in Spokane, built at the lavish cost of a quarter of a million dollars, was for decades the finest theater building in the West.

Today, dozens of small towns have amateur theater groups, while the large cities are home to professional companies. The University of Washington's School of Drama trains young actors and actresses. Drama students also attend classes at Seattle's Cornish College of the Arts.

SPORTS

Outdoor sports such as fishing, hiking, and hunting are a passion in the Evergreen State. Mountain climbing is especially popular, for both Washingtonians and tourists from all over the world. One of the most challenging peaks is lofty, snow-covered Mount Rainier. The first recorded conquest of Mount Rainier was accomplished by Hazard Stevens, son of Territorial Governor Isaac Stevens. Today climbers pack tents and backpacks and take two days to trudge up Rainier's 14,410-foot (4,392-kilometer) slope. Each year, about seven thousand climbers attempt the trek up Mount Rainier; about half that number give up before reaching the top.

Washingtonians have long excelled at winter sports. Skier Gretchen Fraser of Vancouver became one of the first American women to win an Olympic gold medal when she took first place in the giant slalom in the 1948 winter games. In the 1980s, twin brothers Phil and Steve Mahre of White Pass and Debbie Armstrong of Seattle won medals in Olympic skiing events.

A skier in the Alpine Lakes Wilderness

College sports enjoy a loyal following, especially during football season. A strange hush falls over the state when the University of Washington Huskies face their interstate rivals, the Washington State Cougars. During that traditional November game, nearly every Washingtonian is planted firmly in front of a television set, gazing intently at every play.

Basketball's Seattle SuperSonics became Washington's first major-league professional team in 1967. In professional football, the Seattle Seahawks have produced many fine individual performers, but no championship teams. A longtime Seahawk star was sure-handed wide receiver Steve Largent, who set pass-receiving records. The Seattle Mariners of baseball's American League achieved a first during the 1990 season when it acquired veteran Ken Griffey, Sr., father of the Mariners' young star Ken Griffey, Jr. It was the only time in baseball history that a father and son played for the same team.

Chapter 9

A TOUR OF THE EVERGREEN STATE

A TOUR OF THE EVERGREEN STATE

For generations, Washingtonians have worked to maintain their state's scenic marvels as public land open to all. Washington has three national parks, more than a hundred state parks, and nine national forests. Fully one-third of its land area is devoted to parks and public wilderness areas.

In addition to its magnificent world of nature, the state has an urban, sophisticated face. Its cities boast art galleries, museums, and surprising architectural landmarks.

EASTERN WASHINGTON

Washington's northeast corner is covered by the Colville National Forest. In this dense woodland are fifty-five lakes and more than forty streams. Winding through the heart of the forest is the Pend Oreille River, which washes past such towns as Metaline Falls, Tiger, Lost Creek, and Ruby. At the national forest's edge lies the city of Colville, where the Stevens County Historical Museum displays artifacts once owned by the region's early settlers.

Called the "biggest thing built by the hands of man," Grand Coulee Dam is a stellar attraction in eastern Washington. Visitors to the dam ride up a glass elevator to behold a spectacular view of the spillway. The dam itself is nearly a mile (1.6 kilometers) long

The town of
St. John lies
nestled in the
rolling fields
of southeastern
Washington.

and is a major source of hydroelectric power. The 150-mile-
(241-kilometer-) long Franklin D. Roosevelt Lake, which stretches
north to the town of Kettle Falls, was created by the dam.
Vacationers on the lake rent houseboats that sleep up to fourteen
people and are equipped with a water slide and a barbecue pit.

Rich farms and interesting lake country lie south of the dam.
Near the town of Ephrata is Soap Lake, so named because the
early explorers found that its mineral and oil content left their
skin with a soapy feeling. Indians of the area believed that the lake
possessed healing qualities, and sent their sick to drink and bathe
there. Nearby Moses Lake is a gathering place for those who like
to boat and fish.

Spokane, the hub of eastern Washington, features one of the nation's finest park systems. The downtown Riverfront Park—the site of Expo '74—is a popular meeting place. Spokane's Eastern Washington Science Center features 150 hands-on exhibits, as well as a planetarium. The five-story Museum of Native American Cultures gives visitors a unique look at Indian life before the arrival of white pioneers. Another popular museum is the Cheney Cowles Memorial Museum, which has exhibits of Native American and Northwest history. Spokane's massive Cathedral of St. John the Evangelist is a fine example of Gothic church architecture. In a neighborhood called Browne's Addition stand dozens of restored houses that date back to the 1890s.

Pullman, home of Washington State University, lies to the south. On campus is the Connors Museum of Zoology, one of the state's best zoos. The city of Walla Walla calls itself the "cradle of Northwest history" because of its long ties to the region's past. At the Fort Walla Walla Museum Complex, visitors may tour fourteen restored or re-created pioneer buildings, including a log cabin built in 1859. Near Walla Walla is the Whitman Mission National Historic Site, where Marcus and Narcissa Whitman established their mission and were killed during the Cayuse uprising.

The Tri-Cities—Kennewick, Richland, and Pasco—offer visitors historical attractions as well as outdoor excitement. Pioneer and Indian history can be studied at Kennewick's East Benton County Historical Museum and at Pasco's Franklin County Historical Museum. Richland boasts a fine collection of art museums. In the Tri-Cities region is Lake Sacajawea, named after the young Indian woman who helped guide the Lewis and Clark Expedition. Sacajawea State Park is located at the juncture of the Snake and Columbia rivers, where Lewis and Clark camped in 1805.

Lake Chelan, which lies in north-central Washington, is a popular recreation area.

CENTRAL WASHINGTON

Omak and Okanogan are two of north-central Washington's largest towns. Omak is known for its annual Stampede and Suicide Race, in which professional rodeo riders dash their horses down a hill so steep it resembles the side of a cliff. Animal-welfare groups have protested the race because of the possibility the horse could be seriously injured.

The summer-resort town of Chelan sits at the headwaters of Lake Chelan, a long, narrow body of water that on a map looks like a fat worm. The lakeshore offers exciting opportunities for horseback riding. To the south is Wenatchee, whose North Central Washington Museum presents exhibits on pioneer life. Another Wenatchee highlight is the Ohme Gardens, a 9-acre (3.6-hectare) oasis of exotic plant life complete with tiny waterfalls.

Central Washington is apple country. A drive through the region reveals apple orchards on either side of the road. The Wenatchee Valley alone harvests thirty thousand boxcarloads of apples each year. Many orchard owners offer tourists a pick-your-own bargain price on a bushel of apples or pears. While tourists are picking, they may eat as much of the fresh fruit as they like.

The city of Ellensburg is located at the geographical center of Washington. When Washington became a state in 1889, many political leaders believed Ellensburg should have been made its capital because of its central location. However, a terrible fire in the summer of 1889 leveled the town, destroying its chances of becoming the seat of government. Today, Ellensburg is a favorite of rock hounds, who search the surrounding countryside for "Ellensburg Blue" agate, a rare variety of quartz found only in this region.

To the north is a river town with the unusual name Cle Elum. The name is taken from an Indian expression meaning "water running swiftly." Cle Elum welcomes people to Iron Horse State Park, a place of many scenic hiking trails. Near the town of Vantage is Ginkgo Petrified Forest State Park. In the far distant past, this part of central Washington was a wetland that supported gigantic trees. Then, some 20 million years ago, a series of volcanoes erupted, covering the trees with lava. The lava coating turned the ancient forest into pillars of stone. Walking the petrified forest's interpretive trail takes one on a trip into geological history.

The city of Yakima is the center of the agriculturally rich Yakima Valley. This valley owes its productivity to irrigation, as does much of central Washington. Without irrigation water, the land could support little more than scrub grass and sagebrush. Yakima's H. M. Gilbert Homeplace, now a museum, was built in 1898 by one of the region's pioneers in irrigation. The Yakima Valley Museum has a delightful collection of antique horse-drawn vehicles.

The Maryhill Museum of Art stands on a cliff high above the Columbia River.

To the south is the town of Goldendale, gateway to Goldendale Observatory State Park. Perched on a wooded hillside in the park is a gigantic telescope through which visitors are invited to peer into the heavens. It is the nation's largest telescope open for public viewing. South of Goldendale is the splendid Maryhill Museum of Art, which stands on a cliff overlooking the Columbia River.

On the border with Oregon stretches the Columbia River Gorge, one of the most spectacular scenic attractions of the Northwest. The mighty Columbia has worked for centuries here to carve a jagged and lovely canyon out of solid rock. Klickitat Gorge, near the town of Lyle, is a stretch of astonishing bluffs overlooking a tributary of the Columbia. Near North Bonneville rises Beacon Rock, an 800-foot (244-meter) ancient volcano that resembles a gigantic tree jutting out of the hillside. Those rugged enough to climb hiking trails to the highest points of Beacon Rock enjoy a marvelous view of the river gorge.

Mount Baker in the North Cascades

NORTHWEST WASHINGTON

Craggy walls of granite greet visitors to North Cascades
National Park. Hiking trails weave in between the monoliths. The
national park and its surroundings represent nature's Washington,
where there are few towns or other signs of civilization. In fact,
the first major road to this unspoiled region did not open until
1972. To the west is the Mount Baker Wilderness Area, another
lovely, unspoiled tract of forests and mountains. Nearby lies
Rockport State Park, where hiking trails lead through an old-
growth forest.

Bellingham is home to Western Washington University, which
serves some ninety-five hundred students. The city's Whatcom
Museum of History and Art is famous throughout the state.

Fidalgo Island, one of the San Juan Islands

Bellingham is justly proud of its park system, which includes 38-acre (15-hectare) Arroya Park, where hikers trek through scenic canyons.

A visit to the northwest part of the state is incomplete without a trip to the San Juan Islands, which lie in Puget Sound. The San Juan group is made up of 172 islands. Four of them—Lopez, Shaw, Orcas, and San Juan—are accessible by ferryboat from the port city of Anacortes. Visitors to the islands can hike along scenic footpaths and watch seals at play on the rocks below. The islands are also an ideal base for boating, biking, golfing, fishing, and camping. Many artists live and work in the San Juan Islands. Galleries in the town of Friday Harbor, the largest city in the islands, display the work of local artists and craftspeople.

Mount Vernon, founded in 1877 on the anniversary of George Washington's birthday, was named after the first president's Virginia plantation. On farms surrounding the city stretch endless

The International District (left) is one of the many interesting
neighborhoods of Seattle, which lies in Puget Sound (right).

fields of peas. Forty percent of the nation's peas are grown in the
Mount Vernon region. To the south and east are the towns of
Granite Falls and Darrington, which are linked by a scenic road
called the Mountain Loop Highway.

Touring the gigantic Boeing plant, where the latest 747s are
assembled, is a highlight of a visit to Everett. The Boeing Airplane
Company tour center offers visitors a ninety-minute trip through
the factory and a slide show. Young people flock to the Children's
Zoo at Everett's Forest Park.

THE PUGET SOUND AREA

Exciting, booming Seattle is the jewel of Washington's cities.
Even shopping here is an adventure. At the city's Pike Place

More than thirty-five historic aircraft are on display at the Museum of Flight.

Market, where Seattle's freshest fruit, vegetables, and seafood can be found, fishmongers shout out, "Fresh salmon here, look at these beauties!" The city's International District tempts diners with a dizzying assortment of Chinese, Japanese, Filipino, and Korean restaurants. Pioneer Square, on the waterfront, is the city's oldest neighborhood and its cultural heart. Few neighborhoods in the nation offer as many art galleries and storefront bookstores as Pioneer Square.

Visitors often begin a tour of Seattle with a ride on the monorail to the Seattle Center, a 74-acre (30-hectare) development built for the 1962 World's Fair. The observation deck of the Space Needle, which towers more than 500 feet (152 meters) high, provides tourists with a panoramic view of the city. The nearby Pacific Science Center contains more than 120 hands-on exhibits. An African savanna where zebras, lions, and giraffes roam free is re-created at Seattle's Woodland Park Zoo. An outstanding collection of Asian art is on display at the Seattle Art Museum.

Point Defiance Park (left) and Old City Hall (right) are two Tacoma landmarks.

More than thirty-five historic aircraft, including the B-17 bomber of World War II fame, are housed at the Museum of Flight, just south of Seattle.

Seattle's neighbor, Bellevue, is a sophisticated city with many high-tech industries. Bellevue boasts an art museum, a philharmonic orchestra, and several theater companies. Containing more than two hundred stores, Bellevue Square is one of the state's largest shopping malls. Residents also enjoy shopping at Old Bellevue, a restored business center.

Across Puget Sound is the city of Bremerton, an important naval base. Visitors to Bremerton may tour the Naval Shipyard Museum, which holds artifacts of American and Japanese naval history. Bremerton is located on a scenic expanse of land called the Kitsap Peninsula. Nearby attractions include the town of Silverdale, home of the Kitsap Historical Museum; and Poulsbo, a seaside village proud of its Norwegian heritage.

Tacoma's most popular playground is the 700-acre (283-hectare) Point Defiance Park, which features a zoo and a deep-sea aquarium. The park is also home to Fort Nisqually, a replica of an 1832 fur-trading post. Tacoma's Washington State Historical Museum holds one of the finest collections of artifacts from the Evergreen State's past.

In the center of Olympia rises the cluster of government buildings known as the Capital Campus. Towering above all is the legislative building, whose 287-foot (87-meter) dome dominates the skyline. Walking the campus grounds, one is overwhelmed by the lush green grass and colorful flower gardens. The plants for these gardens are grown at the State Greenhouse, which is tucked between the campus buildings. A few blocks from the campus stands the Old State Capitol Building, which served as the seat of government until 1903. The nearby State Capitol Museum contains a special display illustrating how Washington Territory became a state.

SOUTHWEST WASHINGTON

The Indians called Mount Rainier *Tahoma*, a place where the gods resided. The great mountain is still held in awe by the people of Washington. Mount Rainier National Park is the state's single most popular tourist attraction. Visitors hike the parkland's 300 miles (483 kilometers) of trails past glacier-fed rivers, lakes, meadows, and many acres of virgin forests.

Below Mount Rainier rise other giants of the Cascade Range. Mount Adams is popular with backpackers who hike its Pacific Crest National Scenic Trail. Mount St. Helens, which blew its top in 1980, still spews steam. Nevertheless, hikers in the 1990s can spot weeds, vines, and the heads of baby pine trees poking out of

Forested mountains (left) and glacial ice caves (right) are among the natural wonders of Mount Rainier National Park.

the blanket of ash left by the eruption. This struggling growth is proof that in nature, rebirth always follows calamity.

Settlement of the Northwest began in earnest in 1825 when the Hudson's Bay Company established a trading post on the Columbia River at Vancouver. The company built a fort and named John McLoughlin as its presiding officer. This fort, which became the Pacific Northwest's most important wilderness outpost, has been carefully reconstructed. Guides wearing uniforms typical of the 1850s give talks on nineteenth-century life in the Pacific Northwest.

Longview and the neighboring town of Kelso developed as lumbering centers in the early 1900s. Today the cities also serve tourists as jumping-off points for interesting nearby attractions. To the north, the town of Chehalis claims the state's oldest

The Pacific coastline near Long Beach

church. Built in 1858, the Claquato Church has hand-carved pews and a bronze bell that arrived from Boston on a ship that had traveled all the way around Cape Horn in South America. Farther north is Centralia, known for its Antique Mall, nearly eighty antique shops housed in an ornate 1920s Elk Grand Lodge. West of Longview are Cathlamet and Skamokawa, two scenic Columbia River fishing towns.

Above the mouth of the Columbia River stretches Washington's lovely southwestern seashore. The town of Ilwaco is a port where deep-water fishermen charter boats and venture into the Pacific to hook salmon. Bird-watching is a prime activity at Leadbetter State Park near the town of Long Beach. Snowy plovers and black brants are among the species that glide over this seaside area. Nearby is Cape Disappointment, so named by explorer John Meares in 1788, who was disappointed when the sea channel he discovered failed to be the Northwest Passage. Few visitors to the southwest coast are disappointed today.

103

Left: Sea stacks along the coast in Olympic National Park
Right: Hoquiam's "Castle," the restored mansion of a Hoquiam lumber tycoon

Aberdeen and Hoquiam are the two largest towns along the bay
known as Grays Harbor. In 1989, the citizens of Aberdeen
celebrated Washington's centennial by building a replica of
Captain Robert Gray's ship *Lady Washington*. The ship now stands
proudly at Aberdeen's harbor entrance. Hoquiam's Polson
Museum contains relics of Grays Harbor's past.

THE OLYMPIC PENINSULA

"The mountains seem to rise from the edge of the water, as
though nature had designed to shut up this spot for her safe
retreat forever." This statement was written about the Olympic
Peninsula in 1888 by Eugene Semple, Washington's territorial

governor. Now, more than a hundred years later, the forested Olympic Mountains remain nature's realm, relatively untouched by humans. Highways skirt the Olympic National Forest, but none penetrate it. The region resisted exploration until the twentieth century, and some of its land remains unexplored to this day.

The 900,000-acre (364,221-hectare) Olympic National Park sprawls over the interior of the Olympic Peninsula. More than 3 million people visit the park each year, but its land area is so large and rugged that hikers trekking along its 600 miles (966 kilometers) of trails rarely encounter one another. Logging and hunting are forbidden on the park grounds, ensuring that the area remains a special retreat for nature lovers. Such rarely seen animals as the Roosevelt elk and the mountain goat live undisturbed within the park boundaries.

Moss-covered Douglas firs rise like cathedrals in the rain forests on the western slope of the mountains. Some of these giants tower higher than a fifteen-story office building. Vast tracts of the woodland are old growth and have stood like monuments for more than seven centuries. Donald Culross, in his book *The Nature of Things*, wrote, "The Olympic Forests are what you imagined virgin forests were when you were a child. They are as tall as trees of a fairy tale, and as dense as that."

Lakes and rivers abound in Olympic National Park. Snaking through the heart of the rain forest is the Hoh River, which is always gushing, thanks to the region's 140-inch- (356-centimeter-) per-year rainfall. The Rain Forest Trail winds along the Hoh's banks, challenging hikers. Lake Crescent is a pristine mountain lake in the north that geologists claim was created in ancient times when a landslide dammed up the Lyre River. The Clallam Indians, however, who have lived in the area for centuries, tell a different version of the lake's creation. According to Native American lore,

Port Townsend boasts the
state's finest collection
of Victorian houses.

the storm god grew enraged at the Clallam people because they
waged war too often. The god hurled a mountain at the tribe, and
boulders jammed the river, giving birth to the lake.

Towering above all other peaks in the Olympic chain is lofty
Mount Olympus. One of thirty-five mountains in the chain that
rise 7,000 feet (2,134 meters) or more, Olympus has long been
queen of the peninsula. In 1788, when explorer John Meares first
saw the lovely peak, he said, "If that be not the home where dwell
the gods, it certainly is beautiful enough to be, and I therefore will
call it Mt. Olympus."

The Olympic Peninsula's rugged coastline is where the region's
few cities are found. Hoodsport is a boating center that sends
pleasure craft into the long and narrow Hood Canal. Historic Port
Townsend, which has the state's finest collection of Victorian
houses, sits on the northwest corner of the peninsula. Port Angeles

An island off the northwest tip of the Olympic Peninsula

is the largest town on the peninsula's north coast. An observation tower that rises over Port Angeles's pier provides a breathtaking view of the sea and the Olympic Mountains. Tiny villages and resort towns such as Ocean City, Moclips, and Queets hug the Pacific coast. Most of the peninsula's Pacific side is made up of windswept cliffs sculpted by the incessant pounding of huge waves.

On the Olympic Peninsula's northwestern tip sits Neah Bay, part of the Makah Indian Reservation. Native Americans have lived on this seaside for thousands of years. The Makah Cultural and Research Center displays objects of their ancient civilization. Neah Bay is an ideal spot to end a tour of Washington. It is a place where the sea meets the earth and the past meets the present. The future is there too—spreading inland. A future of growth and fulfilled dreams continously unfolds in the welcoming state of Washington.

FACTS AT A GLANCE

GENERAL INFORMATION

Statehood: November 11, 1889, forty-second state

Origin of Name: Named for George Washington, first U.S. president

State Capital: Olympia

State Nickname: Evergreen State

State Flag: The state flag consists of the state seal centered on a dark-green field. The seal contains a portrait of George Washington surrounded by the words "The Seal of the State of Washington 1889"

State Motto: *Alki*, a Chinook word meaning "by-and-by"

State Bird: Willow goldfinch

State Flower: Coast rhododendron

State Tree: Western hemlock

State Fish: Steelhead trout

State Gem: Petrified wood

State Colors: Green and gold

State Dance: Square dance

State Song: "Washington, My Home," words and music by Helen Davis:

> Washington, my home
> Wherever I may roam
> This is my land, my native land
> Washington, my home.
>
> Our verdant forest green
> Caressed by silv'ry stream
> From mountain peak
> To fields of wheat
> Washington, my home.

There's peace you feel and understand
In this, our own beloved land.
We greet the day with head held high
And forward ever is our cry.
We'll happy ever be
As people always free
For you and me a destiny;
Washington, my home.

POPULATION

Population: 4,132,204, nineteenth among the states (1980 census)

Population Density: 61 persons per sq. mi. (23 persons per km²)

Population Distribution: Nearly three-fourths of the state's residents live in cities or towns. Most Washington residents live in the Puget Sound area, in cities such as Seattle, Tacoma, Bellevue, and Everett. Spokane, in eastern Washington, is the largest city outside of the Seattle-Tacoma area.

Seattle	493,846
Spokane	171,300
Tacoma	158,501
Bellevue	73,903
Everett	54,413
Yakima	49,826
Bellingham	45,794
Vancouver	42,834
Bremerton	36,208
Kennewick	34,397

(Population figures according to 1980 census)

Population Growth: The list below shows population growth in Washington since 1850:

Year	Population
1850	1,201
1870	23,955
1890	357,232
1900	518,103
1910	1,141,990
1920	1,356,621
1930	1,563,396
1940	1,736,191
1950	2,378,963
1960	2,853,214
1970	3,413,244
1980	4,132,204

Pike Place Market in Seattle

GEOGRAPHY

Borders: Washington is bordered by Idaho on the east, Oregon on the south, the Pacific Ocean on the west, and the Canadian province of British Columbia on the north.

Highest Point: Mount Rainier, 14,410 ft. (4,392 m)

Lowest Point: Sea level, at the Pacific Ocean

Greatest Distances: North to south—239 mi. (385 km)
East to west—370 mi. (595 km)

Area: 68,139 sq. mi. (176,480 km²)

Rank in Area Among the States: Twentieth

Indian Reservations: About 35,000 of Washington's 105,574 Native Americans reside on reservation land set aside by the federal government. Washington's twenty-six reservations, located throughout the state, are Chehalis, Colville, Hoh, Jamestown Clallam, Kalispel, Lower Elwha, Lummi, Makah, Muckleshoot, Nisqually, Nooksack, Port Gamble, Port Madison, Puyallup, Quileute, Quinault, Sauk-Suiattle, Shoalwater, Skokomish, Spokane, Squaxin Island, Stillaguamish, Swinomish, Tulalip, Upper Skagit, and Yakima.

National Parks and Forests: More than a third of Washington is covered by national forest or national parkland. Some of the most beautiful land in the nation is found within Washington's three national parks. Olympic National Park, on the

111

Sunset on Fidalgo Island

Olympic Peninsula, is a mountainous, glacier-clad, densely forested wilderness area that includes a lush rain forest and a long strip of rugged Pacific coastland. Mount Rainier National Park surrounds the majestic mountain that is the highest peak in the Cascades. North Cascades National Park, near the Canadian border, contains jagged peaks, canyons, rivers, and lakes. Mount St. Helens, which had a massive eruption in 1980, is now protected as a national monument. Washington has nine national forests; seven of these—Gifford Pinchot, Mount Baker, Snoqualmie, Wenatchee, Olympic, Colville, and Okanogan—are located entirely within the state. Kaniksu National Forest is shared with Idaho and Montana; Umatilla National Forest is shared with Oregon. The state also has several national wilderness and recreation areas.

Rivers: Most of the state's major rivers flow into the Columbia, which forms much of the Washington-Oregon border and empties into the Pacific Ocean west of Longview. The Snake River, which wiggles through eastern Washington, Idaho, and Wyoming, is the largest of the Columbia's tributaries. Other major tributaries of the Columbia include the Yakima, Spokane, Okanogan, Sanpoil, Pend Oreille, Lewis, and Cowlitz. Several smaller rivers flow from sources in the Cascade Mountains to Puget Sound. These include the Nooksack, Skagit, Stillaguamish, Skykomish, Cedar, Puyallup, and Nisqually.

Lakes: Washington has about a thousand natural lakes, many of them the result of mountain glaciers. Largest of these natural lakes is stringbean-shaped Lake

112

Autumn in the Cascade Mountains

Chelan, which is about 55 mi. (89 km) long but only 1 to 3 mi. (1.6 to 5 km) wide. In many places, this lake is more than 1,500 ft. (457 m) deep. Lake Washington, which forms Seattle's eastern border, provides water and recreation for the city. Crescent, Cushman, Quinault, and Ozette are important lakes on the Olympic Peninsula. Large lakes in the Cascades include Wenatchee, Kachess, Keechelus, and Cle Elum. Moses and Soap lakes are the largest natural lakes in the Columbia Basin area. Washington also has many artificial lakes formed by damming the state's rivers. Largest of these is Franklin D. Roosevelt Lake, created by Grand Coulee Dam on the Columbia River.

Coasts: As the crow flies, Washington has 157 mi. (253 km) of coastline. However, including the outer coast, bays, rivers, creeks, and offshore islands, Washington's coastline spreads 3,026 mi. (4,870 km). Only eight other states have more shoreline than Washington.

Topography: Few states have the physical variety of Washington, a land of mountains, plateaus, and lowlands. Four different mountain regions alone are found in the state. The Rocky Mountains cut into the northeastern corner, north of the Spokane River and east of the Okanogan River. West of the Spokane, the Cascade Mountains cut through and dominate the central part of the state. Southwest Washington is part of the Coast Range, high mountains that extend all the way to California. A fourth range, the picturesque Olympic Mountains, covers most of the Olympic Peninsula.

The region known as the Puget Sound Lowland extends east of Puget Sound, west to the Pacific between the Coast Range and Olympic Mountains, and south to Oregon. The cities of Seattle, Tacoma, Bellevue, Everett, Bellingham, Olympia, and Vancouver are located in this region. Southeastern Washington is part of a large basin called the Columbia Plateau. This semi-arid plateau contains several of Washington's important cities, including Spokane, Yakima, and Walla Walla.

Climate: The high, rugged Cascade Mountains create a formidable barrier between western and eastern Washington and have a great effect on the state's weather. Washingtonians living west of the Cascades get frequent showers from Pacific Ocean clouds. Moist air sweeping in from the Pacific is deflected upward as it encounters the mountains. As the ocean air rises, it loses moisture in the form of rainfall. Consequently, the western, or Pacific, side of the mountains receives far more rainfall than the eastern side. These rains come on warm Pacific winds that prevent the moisture from turning into snow. The Olympic Peninsula averages 135 in. (343 cm) of precipitation per year. But snowfall averages a mere 5 in. (13 cm) along the coast. The warm winds give Seattle a winter climate more comfortable than that of most northern cities; January temperatures average about 41° F. (5° C). The Pacific winds also help Seattle's summers stay relatively cool; July temperatures there average 66° F. (19° C).

The part of the state lying east of the Cascades receives little precipitation and is warmer in the summer and colder in the winter than western Washington. The central plateau may receive only about 6 in. (15 cm) of precipitation per year. Spokane, on the eastern plateau, has an average January temperature of 21° F. (-6° C) and an average July temperature of 70° F. (21° C).

Ice Harbor Dam, in southeastern Washington, recorded the state's highest temperature—a sweltering 118° F. (48° C)—on August 5, 1961. Residents of Mazama and Winthrop shivered when their thermometers fell to the all-time state low of -48° F. (-44° C) on December 30, 1968. Paradise Ranger Station on Mount Rainier recorded 1,027 in. (2,609 cm) of snow during the winter of 1970-71—the heaviest snowfall in one season ever recorded in the U.S.

NATURE

Trees: Douglas fir, ponderosa pine, Sitka spruce, western hemlock, western red cedar, western larch, lodgepole pine, alder, aspen, cottonwood, maple

Wild Plants: Brown-eyed Susan, goldenrod, lupine, western rhododendron, monkey flower, mountain phlox, heather, lace, fern, shooting star, Flett's violet, piper bluebell, sea rose, moss, Oregon grape, sagebrush, sunflower, everlasting lily, wild onion

Animals: Deer, beaver, marten, mink, muskrat, bobcat, crab, oyster, clam, gopher, mountain lion, mountain goat, badger, marmot, flying squirrel, seal, sea lion

Bagley Creek in Snoqualmie National Forest

Birds: Pheasant, quail, ruffed grouse, western lark, sage grouse, duck, goose, owl, hawk, falcon, vireo, waxwing, shrike, goldfinch, turkey vulture, bald eagle, golden eagle, sandpiper, oystercatcher, gull, tern, swan, cormorant, pelican, turnstone

Fish: Rainbow trout, cutthroat trout, steelhead trout, whitefish, sturgeon, cod, salmon, flounder, halibut, albacore tuna

GOVERNMENT

Washington operates under the state's original constitution, which was adopted in 1889 and has been amended more than seventy-five times. Amendments may be proposed by the state legislature or by a convention called by the legislature and a majority of the state's voters. Amendments must be approved by two-thirds of each house of the legislature, then by a majority of the voters in the statewide election.

The state government, like the federal government, is divided into three branches. The legislative branch consists of a forty-nine-member senate and a ninety-eight-member house of representatives. Voters in each of the forty-nine legislative districts choose one senator and two representatives. Senators serve four-year terms; representatives serve two-year terms. The legislature meets for up

115

The Spokane County Courthouse

Whitman College in Walla Walla

to 90 days in even-numbered years and up to 120 days in odd-numbered years, but the governor may call special legislative sessions.

Washington's executive branch consists of a governor, lieutenant governor, secretary of state, treasurer, attorney general, auditor, superintendent of public instruction, commissioner of public lands, and insurance commissioner. All serve four-year terms and all may be elected an unlimited number of times.

Judicial power rests in the court system. The highest court, the state supreme court, has nine judges elected to six-year terms. Three judges are elected every two years. The judge with the shortest remaining term serves as chief justice. If two or more judges have equal terms remaining, the other judges choose the chief justice. The state's court of appeals has twelve justices elected to six-year terms. District superior courts have one or more justices elected to four-year terms. Justice-of-the-peace courts have justices elected to four-year terms.

Number of Counties: 39

U.S. Representatives: 8

Electoral Votes: 10

Voting Requirements: U.S. citizen, eighteen years of age, resident of the state thirty days before election

EDUCATION

British traders opened the first school in the Washington region in 1832, for children of employees of the Hudson's Bay Company. In the 1840s, in eastern Washington, missionaries Marcus and Narcissa Whitman operated schools for Indian children. Five American schools were operating when the Washington Territory was created in 1853. The territorial legislature immediately passed laws providing for a common school system. The University of Washington, in Seattle, opened its doors in 1861.

An elected superintendent of public instruction administers the public school system. He or she implements the decisions of the state board of education. Twelve members, elected by the directors of local school districts, form this board.

All children between the ages of eight and fifteen are required to attend school. Public schools spend about $3,800 per student each year, well above the national average.

The University of Washington in Seattle is the state's largest institution of higher learning. Other state schools include Washington State University in Pullman, Western Washington University in Bellingham, Central Washington University in Ellensburg, Eastern Washington University in Cheney, and Evergreen State College in Olympia. In addition to the University of Washington, Seattle also boasts four private schools: Cornish College of the Arts, Griffin College, Seattle Pacific University, and Seattle University. Other private schools include City University in Bellevue, Gonzaga University and Whitworth College in Spokane, Lutheran Bible Institute of Seattle in Issaquah, Northwest College of the Assemblies of God in Kirkland, Pacific Lutheran University and University of Puget Sound in Tacoma, St. Martin's College in Lacey, Walla Walla College in College Place, and Whitman College in Walla Walla.

ECONOMY AND INDUSTRY

Principal Products:
Agriculture: Wheat, apples, oats, rye, potatoes, dry beans, green peas, hops, hay, sugar beets, flower bulbs, alfalfa seed, nuts, barley, sheep, beef cattle, dairy cattle, poultry, asparagus, berries, grapes, pears, cherries, plums, prunes, apricots
Manufacturing: Commercial aircraft, ships, transportation equipment, processed foods, machinery, lumber, aluminum, copper, steel, metal products, chemicals, printing and publishing, paper and pulp products, computer software, electronics
Natural Resources: Forests, fish and other seafood, coal, gold, silver, magnesium, lead, zinc, limestone, clay, sand, gravel

Business and Trade: Manufacturing is the state's leading industry, and transportation equipment accounts for most of the state's manufacturing activity. The Boeing Company, headquartered in Seattle, leads the nation in airplane construction. The Puget Sound Naval Shipyard at Bremerton builds naval vessels and repairs much of the American fleet. Food-processing plants, another important part of the state's economy, produce such varied items as canned salmon, frozen fruit, flour, and dairy products. Washington's vast timber resources are converted into many different products, including furniture, shingles, and paper products.

Offshore fishermen net more than two hundred species of fish and seafood. Salmon is the most important catch. Other commercial fish include halibut, cod, ocean perch, sole, and flounder. Fishermen also "harvest" clams, oysters, and crabs.

Seattle and Tacoma are vital shipping centers to growing Asian markets. They are among only six American cities where goods may be brought in duty-free. Seattle and Tacoma also serve as gateways and marketing centers for oil- and mineral-rich Alaska. Anacortes, on Puget Sound, and Vancouver, on the Columbia River, are other important ports. Spokane, at the other end of the state, serves as the commercial hub of the "Inland Empire."

Communication: The *Columbian*, published at Olympia in 1852, was the first Washington newspaper. The state now has about 25 daily newspapers and 130 weeklies. The *Seattle Post-Intelligencer* and *Seattle Times*, both of Seattle, are the most widely read newspapers. Other important dailies include the *Tacoma News-Tribune* and Spokane's *SpokesmanReview*.

KFBL (now KRKO) of Everett went on the air as the first Washington radio station in 1920. Today, the state has about 200 radio stations. KING of Seattle, the first of 20 television stations now broadcast in Washington, began operations in 1948.

Transportation: Rivers, the ocean, and Puget Sound served as Washington's first "highways." Even today, these waterways are important. Barges chug down the Columbia River bearing goods for shipment. The Lake Washington Ship Canal, which runs through Seattle and connects Lake Washington with Puget Sound, handles more than 2 million tons (1.8 million metric tons) of cargo each year. The Snohomish River, Lake Chelan, and Franklin D. Roosevelt Lake also see extensive cargo. Washington has an outstanding state ferry system that serves Puget Sound, the San Juan Islands, Vancouver Island, and the Olympic Peninsula.

Railroads led the way in connecting Washington to the East. The Northern Pacific, Great Northern, Milwaukee, and other lines brought in the settlers that made statehood possible. Today, Washington has about 4,100 mi. (6,598 km) of track. Fifteen lines deliver freight, and there are passenger stops in thirteen cities. The 7.8-mi. (12.5-km) Cascade Tunnel, the longest railroad tunnel in the Western Hemisphere, was completed in 1929.

Highways, though late in coming, now cover much of the state. Interstate Highway 5, which enters Washington at Vancouver, is a major north-south route that runs through the Puget Sound cities before reaching the Canadian border. Interstate 90, a major east-west route across the central part of the state, connects Spokane and Seattle. Interstate 82 starts near Kennewick and ends near Ellensburg. Altogether, the state has about 70,000 mi. (112,651 km) of paved roads.

Washington's relative distance from the rest of America makes air travel important in the state. Seattle-Tacoma International Airport is the major airport in the Pacific Northwest. Other major airports are located in Spokane, Yakima, and Walla Walla. Washington has about 375 airports.

SOCIAL AND CULTURAL LIFE

Museums: Washingtonians, with their rich and varied traditions, honor their history and culture in many museums. The Washington State Historical Society in Tacoma contains the state's largest history museum. Olympia's State Capitol Museum contains historical and Native American materials, an art gallery, and a natural-history museum. Seattle's Museum of History and Industry traces the development of Washington settlement and industries. Spokane boasts the Museum of Native American Cultures and the Cheney Cowles Memorial Museum, which features an art gallery and exhibits on Native American and Northwest history. The Lewis County Historical Museum in Chehalis preserves pioneer and Indian artifacts and an old cemetery. Adam East Museum in Moses Lake displays prehistoric artifacts. Thomas Burke Memorial State Museum at the University of Washington has an extensive collection of Indian artifacts.

Science enthusiasts also have many choices. The Pacific Science Center in Seattle includes exhibits on modern scientific discoveries, a planetarium, and laser shows. Eastern Washington University has a planetarium as well. The Hanford Science Center in Richland features exhibits relating to energy and the environment. The Seattle Aquarium has a 400,000-gallon (1.5 million-liter) underwater dome with re-created Puget Sound habitats.

Art lovers enjoy the world-renowned Oriental art and jade collection at the Seattle Art Museum. European and American art is on display at the Charles and Emma Frye Art Museum at Seattle. The Henry Art Gallery at the University of Washington features modern art. The Maryhill Museum of Art in Goldendale has large collections of Rodin sculptures, Russian icons, and chess pieces.

Other interesting museums in Washington include the Bremertown Naval Museum, which presents navy and shipyard history; and Seattle's Museum of Flight, which explores the history of aviation in the Pacific Northwest. Gonzaga University in Seattle has a library and memorabilia donated by its most famous alumnus, singer and actor Bing Crosby.

Libraries: The Territorial Library, Washington's first library, opened in Olympia in 1853 to serve legislators and territorial officials. Now called the State Library, it contains thousands of state documents. The University of Washington has the largest library in the state. North Central Regional Library in Wenatchee is one of the largest single libraries in the country. The Seattle Public Library is known for its materials on the Pacific Northwest and aeronautics. The first Washington public library opened in Steilacoom in 1858. Today, the state has about eighty public libraries and library systems.

Performing Arts: The Seattle Center Opera House, in Seattle Center, is the home of several fine performing arts organizations, including the Seattle Symphony Orchestra, one of the nation's finest symphony orchestras; the well-respected Seattle Youth Symphony; and The Seattle Opera Association. One of the nation's most highly acclaimed repertory theater companies, the Seattle Repertory Theater, performs at Bagley Wright Theatre, also in Seattle Center. Among Seattle's other theater groups are A Contemporary Theater (ACT), which presents contemporary

Participants in the annual Seattle to Portland Bicycle Ride

works; and The Empty Space, which presents contemporary and experimental plays. Seattle's Pacific Northwest Ballet is a professional resident ballet company. The University of Washington has a highly respected school of drama. Cornish College of the Arts offers instruction and programs in music and other arts. Other colleges and universities also present varied performances throughout the year. Each year, the state's artists and authors are honored at the annual Governor's Festival of the Arts in Olympia.

Sports and Recreation: Seattle hosts the Mariners of baseball's American League, the Seahawks of the National Football League, and the SuperSonics of the National Basketball Association. The Tacoma Stars compete in the Major Indoor Soccer League. Hockey fans in the Seattle area may follow the National Hockey League's Vancouver Canucks. The sports teams of the University of Washington and Washington State University belong to the Pacific Ten, one of the strongest conferences in the nation. The Seattle area is famous for its hydroplane races.

Washington's vast, beautiful parklands offer nearly unlimited opportunities for hiking, hunting, camping, boating, rafting, horseback riding, sailing, fishing, bicycling, mountain-climbing, snowmobiling, waterskiing, downhill skiing, and cross-country skiing.

Historic Sites and Landmarks:

Ebey's Landing National Historical Reserve, on Whidbey Island, preserves a rural settlement founded in the 1850s and two historic forts.

Fort Spokane, near Grand Coulee Dam, was an army outpost that was built in 1880 to keep peace between settlers and Indians. Four of the fort's original buildings still remain.

Fort Vancouver National Historical Site, in Vancouver, is a reconstruction of the western headquarters of the Hudson's Bay Company.

Hoquiam's "Castle," a national historic site in Hoquiam, is a beautifully restored mansion that was built by lumber tycoon Robert Lytle.

Klondike Gold Rush National Historical Park, in Seattle's Pioneer Square, honors Seattle's role in the Klondike gold rush. It is the southern unit of a park headquartered in Skagway, Alaska.

Monticello Convention Site, in Longview, marks the spot where residents of Washington petitioned the federal government to separate Washington from Oregon.

Mount St. Helens National Volcanic Monument is the site of the violent 1980 volcanic eruption that killed sixty people and made headlines around the world.

Pioneer Square Historic District, Seattle's oldest neighborhood, is an eighteen-block area of carefully restored historic buildings, many of which house elegant restaurants, shops, and art galleries.

Port Gamble is a well-preserved mill town that was established in 1863. A national historic landmark, it features restored homes, a museum, and a company store.

San Juan Island National Historic Park, on San Juan Island, commemorates the bloodless dispute that occurred when both the U.S. and Britain laid claim to San Juan Island following the Oregon Treaty of 1846.

Whitman Mission National Historic Site, near Walla Walla, commemorates the Indian mission founded in 1836 by Marcus and Narcissa Whitman.

Other Interesting Places to Visit:

Capitol Campus, in Olympia, includes the legislative building, temple of justice, administrative buildings, and well-manicured grounds with Japanese cherry trees.

Grand Coulee Dam, in north-central Washington, is one of the world's largest hydroelectric facilities and the largest concrete structure in the U.S.

Hell's Canyon, a spectacular gorge on the Snake River in southeastern Washington, is the deepest canyon in the continental U.S.

Holland Gardens, in Oak Harbor, contains acres of flowers and shrubs surrounding a blue-and-white windmill.

Monorail, built in Seattle for the 1962 world's fair, was the first one-rail train in the nation. It links Seattle Center with the downtown area.

Mount Rainier, the state's highest peak, towers over scenic Mount Rainier National Park.

Old Capitol Building, in Olympia, is famous for its Romanesque architecture.

Palouse River Canyon, near Dayton, contains a deeply eroded gorge and cliffs that rise hundreds of feet above the river.

Peace Arch State Park, in Blaine, is the site of a six-story-high arch that stretches across the U.S.-Canadian border to commemorate more than a century of friendship between Canada and the United States.

Pike Place Market, in Seattle, is a huge farmer's market with a colorful array of seafood, fruits, vegetables, and spices.

Point Defiance Park, in Tacoma, has a zoo, flower gardens, a South Pacific aquarium, an outdoor museum of early logging equipment, and Fort Nisqually, a restored Hudson's Bay Company fur-trading post.

San Juan Islands, in Puget Sound, are known for their picturesque beauty.

Space Needle, in Seattle, is a 607-ft. (185-m), 360-degree observation tower that was built for the 1962 world's fair.

Tillicum Village, on Blake Island, offers tours of an Indian longhouse and an authentic coastal Native American feast that includes salmon cooked over a fire, Tillicum hot bread, and wild blackberry cream tarts.

Woodland Park, in Seattle, is a world-class zoo.

IMPORTANT DATES

1775—Bruno Hezeta and Juan Francisco de la Bodega y Quadra become the first known Europeans to land on Washington soil

1778—Captain James Cook becomes the first British explorer to sail along the Washington coast

1787—Charles Barclay sails through the strait between present-day Washington and Vancouver Island and names it for Juan de Fuca

1790—Spain yields its claims in the Northwest to England

1792—British captain George Vancouver surveys the Washington coast and Puget Sound; American captain Robert Gray sails into Grays Harbor and reaches the mouth of the Columbia River

1805—Meriwether Lewis and William Clark follow the Columbia River to the Pacific Ocean

1810—The British-owned North West Company establishes a fur-trading post near present-day Spokane

1811—Canadian explorer David Thompson explores the Columbia River to the Pacific, strengthening British claims to the region; a group led by John Jacob Astor establishes Fort Okanogan, the first permanent American settlement in present-day Washington

1818—Britain and the U.S. agree to a joint occupation of the Oregon Country

1825—John McLoughlin of the British-owned Hudson's Bay Company establishes Fort Vancouver at the site of present-day Vancouver

1832—The first schools in present-day Washington open at Fort Vancouver

1836—Marcus and Narcissa Whitman found an Indian mission near present-day Walla Walla

1844—"Fifty Four-Forty or Fight!", a battle cry demanding that Britain give up its claim to the Oregon land south of 54° 40' north latitude, becomes a presidential campaign issue that helps elect Democrat James Knox Polk

1846—A treaty between Britain and the U.S. establishes as American territory all land south of the 49th parallel—Washington's present boundary with Canada

1847—The Cayuse War is sparked after Cayuse Indians massacre the Whitmans and twelve other mission residents

1848—A bill creating Oregon Territory, which includes the land of present-day Washington, passes Congress

1852—Olympia's *Columbian*, Washington's first newspaper, begins publication

1853—Washington Territory, a territory including present-day Washington, northern Idaho, and western Montana, is created by Congress; the Territorial Library in Olympia, Washington's first library, opens

1855—The discovery of gold in northeastern Washington prompts a rush of prospectors and settlers to the area, triggering strife between the Indians of the region and the white newcomers

1858—Indians lose a battle near Four Lakes, ending three years of intermittent Indian wars in the Washington Territory

1859—Washington Territory expands to include the southern parts of present-day Idaho and Wyoming

1861—The University of Washington holds its first classes

1863—Congress creates Idaho Territory, giving Washington its present boundaries

1866—The first salmon cannery in the Pacific Northwest opens at Eagle Cliff

1871—The first quartz lode in Washington is discovered at Conconully

1883—The Northern Pacific Railroad links Washington with the East Coast; Washington's first paper and pulp mill is built on the Columbia River at Camas

1885—The labor union known as the Knights of Labor takes advantage of prejudice against low-wage Chinese laborers to organize anti-Chinese riots in the Seattle area

1889—Washington is admitted to the Union as the forty-second state; a fire rips through downtown Seattle

1897-98—Seattle merchants and shippers, as well as farmers in eastern Washington, benefit greatly from the Klondike gold rush in Alaska and the Yukon Territory, as Seattle becomes the main supply point for the prospectors

1905—Loggers and transit workers form the organization Industrial Workers of the World

1909—Seattle hosts the Alaska-Yukon-Pacific Exposition

1910—Washington becomes the fifth American state to extend voting rights to women; Spokane resident Sonora Louise Smart Dodd originates Father's Day

1917—The Lake Washington Ship Canal opens

1919—Some sixty thousand protesting workers walk off their jobs in what becomes known as the ''Seattle Revolution of 1919,'' the first general strike in the U.S.; Boeing Company, today one of the world's largest aircraft manufacturers, begins operations in Seattle

1935—Washingtonian Audrey May Wurdemann wins the Pulitzer Prize in poetry for *Bright Ambush*

Grand Coulee Dam was completed in 1942.

1942—Grand Coulee Dam, the largest dam in the world at the time, is completed

1943—An atomic-energy center, used to help make the first atomic bombs, is opened by the federal government at Hanford

1948—Seattle's KING-TV becomes the first Washington television station

1954—Washingtonian Theodore Roethke wins the Pulitzer Prize in poetry for *The Waking*; a $40-million oil refinery opens at Ferndale

1962—Seattle hosts the Century 21 world's fair and introduces the first monorail system in the U.S.

1964—The U.S. and Canadian governments give final approval to a cooperative plan for hydroelectric and river-control projects on the Columbia River

1968—Seattle-area voters approve "Forward Thrust," a $333-million city-improvement program

1970—A slump in the aerospace industry results in the loss of thousands of Seattle-area jobs

1971—The greatest recorded snowfall in the U.S. in one season—1,027 in. (2,609 cm)—occurs at Paradise Ranger station on Mount Rainier

1974—Expo '74, an environment-oriented world's fair, is held in Spokane

1976—Dixy Lee Ray is elected Washington's first woman governor

1979—The U.S. Supreme Court upholds a decision granting Native Americans the right to harvest half of the salmon returning to off-reservation waters in Washington

1980—Mount St. Helens erupts, killing sixty people and vast numbers of wildlife, flattening thousands of acres of forest, spreading volcanic ash over a large area of southwestern Washington, and filling lakes and rivers with mud and debris

1982—Hood Canal Bridge, a vital link between Jefferson County and Kitsap County, reopens

1989—Washington celebrates its centennial; Seattle elects Norman Rice as its first African-American mayor

1990—Seattle hosts the Goodwill Games, a worldwide athletic competition

IMPORTANT PEOPLE

BROCK ADAMS

Brock Adams (1927-   ), politician; U.S. representative from Washington (1965-77); U.S. secretary of transportation under President Jimmy Carter (1977-79); U.S. senator (1987-   )

Earl Averill (1902-1983), born in Snohomish; professional baseball player; starred with the Cleveland Indians and Detroit Tigers; retired with a .318 lifetime batting average; elected to Baseball Hall of Fame (1975)

Dorsey Syng Baker (1823-1888), banker and railroad executive; opened up the Walla Walla area to trade by building a railroad from Walla Walla to the Columbia River town of Wallula

Richard Achilles Ballinger (1858-1922), lawyer, politician; mayor of Seattle (1904-06); served as U.S. secretary of the interior under President William Taft (1909-11); but resigned after foes charged that he opposed conservation policies

Robert William (Bob) Barker (1923-), born in Darrington; television personality; hosted the popular daytime television programs "Truth or Consequences" and "The Price Is Right"; longtime master of ceremonies of the Miss Universe and Miss U.S.A. beauty pageants and the Tournament of Roses Parade; champion of animal-rights causes

William Edward Boeing (1881-1956), engineer, industrialist; pioneered aerospace technology; in 1916 founded the Boeing Airplane Company; based in Seattle since 1919, it is now one of the world's largest airplane manufacturers

Robert William (Bobby) Brown (1924-), born in Seattle; professional baseball player, physician, baseball executive; played third base with the New York Yankees and hit .439 in four World Series; practiced cardiology in Fort Worth, Texas (1958-84); president of baseball's American League (1984-)

Dyan Cannon (1937-), born in Tacoma; actress; starred in such films as *Bob and Carol and Ted and Alice*, *Heaven Can Wait*, and *Revenge of the Pink Panther*

JoAnne Gunderson Carner (1939-), born in Kirkland; golfer; won the U.S. Amateur championship five times; won more than forty LPGA events; entered Women's Sports Foundation Hall of Fame

Carol Channing (1923-), born in Seattle; actress, singer; starred in such Broadway musicals as *Gentlemen Prefer Blondes* and *Hello Dolly!*, for which she won a Tony Award in 1964; appeared in many films, including *The First Traveling Saleslady* and *Thoroughly Modern Millie*

Harry Lillis (Bing) Crosby (1903-1977), born in Tacoma; singer, actor; as a "crooner," sold millions of records, including "White Christmas," the best-selling record of all time; starred in many films, including *Holiday Inn*, *Bells of St. Mary's*, and *Going My Way*, for which he won an Academy Award for best actor (1944); also starred with Bob Hope in a series of "Road" movies

George Robert (Bob) Crosby (1913-), born in Spokane; big-band leader; brother of Bing Crosby; headed "Bob Crosby and the Bobcats" on radio and television

Arthur Armstrong Denny (1822-1899), pioneer, industrialist, author; founded the settlement that became Seattle; helped promote Seattle's growth by working for roads and industrial development linking Seattle to inland towns; wrote *Pioneer Days on Puget Sound.*

RICHARD BALLINGER

BOBBY BROWN

CAROL CHANNING

BING CROSBY

WILLIAM DOUGLAS

JOHN EHRLICHMAN

JOHN ELWAY

GRETCHEN FRASER

Elinor Donahue (1937-   ), born in Tacoma; actress; starred in many early television comedies, including "Father Knows Best," "The Andy Griffith Show," and "Many Happy Returns"

William Orville Douglas (1898-1980), jurist; grew up in Washington; professor of law at Yale University (1928-36); chairman of the Securities and Exchange Commission (1937-39); served the longest term in history as an associate justice of the U.S. Supreme Court (1939-75); worked to protect civil rights and liberties; traveled extensively and wrote books about conservation

Howard Duff (1917-1990), born in Bremerton, actor; known for his rich, deep voice; starred in such films as *Brute Force*, *Naked City*, and *All My Sons*

John Daniel Ehrlichman (1925-   ), born in Tacoma; government official, author; domestic advisor to President Richard M. Nixon; resigned after being implicated in the Watergate scandal; was convicted of conspiracy and obstruction of justice; wrote *The Company*, a thinly disguised novel on Washington, D.C., government

John Elway (1960-   ), born in Port Angeles; professional football player; quarterback who led the Denver Broncos to the Super Bowl in 1987 and 1988

Daniel J. Evans (1925-   ), born in Seattle; politician; governor of Washington (1965-77), U.S. senator (1983-   ); backed the Washington Wilderness Bill and led moves for improved trade with Pacific nations

Elisha P. Ferry (1825-1895), first governor of the state of Washington (1889-93)

Thomas Stephen Foley (1929-   ), born in Spokane; politician; U.S. representative from Washington (1965-   ); House majority leader (1987-89); Speaker of the House (1989-   ); known for his fairmindedness and evenhandedness when dealing with both Democrats and Republicans

Gretchen Claudia Fraser (1919-   ), born in Tacoma; world-class skier; won gold and silver medals in the 1948 Olympics, becoming the first American to win alpine medals; managed the U.S. Women's Olympic team in 1952; worked to promote the Special Winter Olympics

Spokan Garry (1811-1892), born in present-day Spokane County; Spokane Indian chief, missionary; introduced Christianity to his people; started one of the first Indian schools; leader of the Spokane Indians of the Columbia River Basin for nearly sixty years; maintained friendly relations with white settlers and aided peaceful settlement of the region

Slade Gorton (1928-   ), politician; U.S. senator from Washington (1981-87, 1989-   ); as senator, championed environmental measures, pushing passage of an important wilderness act

James Marshall (Jimi) Hendrix (1942-1970), born in Seattle; musician, composer; won acclaim for his guitar playing and the innovative sounds he produced; wrote the songs "Purple Haze," "Fire," and "Hey, Joe"

James Jerome Hill (1838-1916), industrialist; earned the nickname "Empire Builder" for helping unite the Pacific Coast with the Great Lakes; in 1850, founded the Great Northern Railway, the first transcontinental railway constructed without government help, from Lake Superior to Puget Sound

Henry Martin "Scoop" Jackson (1912-1983), born in Everett; politician; U.S. representative from Washington (1941-53); U.S. senator (1953-83); having a reputation for being liberal in domestic matters and conservative in foreign policy, he supported environmental and civil-rights legislation and a strong defense; ran unsuccessfully for president in 1972 and 1976

Robert Joffrey (1930-1988), born Abdullah Jaffa Bey Khan in Seattle; modern-dance choreographer; founded and directed the world-famous Joffrey Ballet; commissioned works by modern choreographers and revived twentieth-century classics

Albert Johnson (1900-1966), born in Spokane; jockey, horse trainer; won more than five hundred races between 1917 and 1929, including two Kentucky derbies

Chief Joseph (1840?-1904), Nez Perce Indian chief; in 1877, after being told to move from Oregon to reservation land in Idaho, tried to lead his people to safety in Canada; during this retreat, fought off U.S. forces, but finally succumbed to U.S. military strength; spent his last years on the Colville reservation in Washington

Mother Joseph (1823-1902), religious leader; led group of four Catholic nuns into Washington Territory in 1856; established and built many schools and hospitals for orphans, the elderly, and the mentally ill

Kamiakin (1800?-1880), Yakima Indian chief; led his people during the Indian wars of 1855; through his stirring oratory, won the support of nearly two thousand warriors

Bertha Knight Landes (1868-1943), politician; mayor of Seattle (1926-28); was the first woman elected mayor of a large U.S. city; advocated many reforms in government

Steve M. Largent (1954-   ), professional football player; as a wide receiver for the Seattle Seahawks, set the NFL record for passes caught in consecutive games

Gary Larson (1950-   ), born in Tacoma; cartoonist; creator of the nationally syndicated cartoon "The Far Side"

Mary Livingstone (1908-1983), born in Seattle; actress; played the character of Jack Benny's wife (her real-life husband) on "The Jack Benny Show"

JIMI HENDRIX

JAMES HILL

ROBERT JOFFREY

MARY LIVINGSTONE

PHIL MAHRE

MARY McCARTHY

CRAIG T. NELSON

DIXY LEE RAY

Phil Mahre (1957-   ), born in Yakima; skier; silver medalist in the slalom at the 1980 Winter Olympics; winner of the World Cup (1981, 1982, 1983); became the first American to win a gold medal in men's skiing when he won the slalom at the 1984 Winter Olympics; co-wrote *No Hill Too Fast* with his brother, Steve, who won the silver medal in the men's slalom at the 1984 Olympics

Kevin McCarthy (1914-   ), born in Seattle; actor; starred as the hunted doctor in the science-fiction classic *Invasion of the Body Snatchers*; has appeared on a number of television programs, including "Flamingo Road"

Mary McCarthy (1912-1989), born in Seattle; author and critic known for her acerbic wit; wrote novels and short stories, many of which featured strong female characters; also wrote essays, reviews, and memoirs; best-known works include *The Group* and *Memoirs of a Catholic Girlhood*

Darren McGavin (1922-   ), born in Spokane; actor; appeared in many films and starred in several television series, including "Mike Hammer," "Riverboat," and "The Night Stalker"

John McIntyre (1907-   ), born in Spokane; actor; played many supporting roles; appeared in the television series "Wagon Train" and "The Virginian"

John McLoughlin (1784-1857), Canadian fur trader; founded the Hudson's Bay Company trading outpost at Fort Vancouver, the site of present-day Vancouver; was the leading figure of the fur trade in the Pacific Northwest; was revered for his assistance to American settlers

Patrice Munsel (1925-   ), born in Spokane, singer; debuted at New York's Metropolitan Opera at age seventeen; appeared occasionally on Broadway, in films, and on television; hosted television's "Patrice Munsel Show"

Craig T. Nelson (1946-   ), born in Spokane; actor, producer; appeared in such televison series as "How the West Was Won," "Charlie's Angels," and "Coach"; also has appeared in many films, including *Poltergeist* and *Silkwood*; produced a series of fifty-two half-hour films on American artists

Vernon Louis Parrington (1871-1929), author, historian; won the 1928 Pulitzer Prize in history for his book *Main Currents in American Thought*

Dixy Lee Ray (1914-   ), born in Tacoma; politician; marine zoologist at the University of Washington (1945-72); chairman of the U.S. Atomic Energy Commission during the Nixon administration; advocated increased use of nuclear energy; governor of Washington (1977-81); first woman governor in Washington history

Norman Rice (1943-   ), politician; mayor of Seattle (1989-   ); first African American to be elected mayor of Seattle

Jimmy Rodgers (1933-   ), born in Camas; musician; performed such songs as ''Honeycomb'' and ''Kisses Sweeter than Wine''

Theodore Roethke (1908-1963), poet; taught at the University of Washington (1947-63); won the 1954 Pulitzer Prize in poetry for *The Waking; Poems 1903-1953*; his poems dealt with inner life; other poetry collections include *Open House* and *The Far Field*

Ryne Sandburg (1959-   ), born in Spokane; professional baseball player; all-star second baseman who won the National League's Most Valuable Player award in 1984; led the Chicago Cubs to National League Eastern Division titles in 1984 and 1989; hit 30 home runs in 1989

Ronald Edward Santo (1940-   ), born in Seattle; professional baseball player; all-star third baseman with the Chicago Cubs; hit 20 or more homers in a season 10 times; drove in 100 or more runs in a season four times

Seathl (1786-1866), born near present-day Seattle; chief of the Duwamish, Suquamish, and other Indian groups of the Puget Sound area; befriended the early white settlers; signed the Treaty of Point Elliot, which established two Indian reservations in Washington territory; remained loyal to the white settlers during the Indian wars of 1855-58; the city of Seattle is named for him

Smohalla (1815?-1895), born in Washington; prophet, teacher, medicine man; chief of the Wanapum, a group that lived in present-day Yakima County; founded the Dreamer religious cult, which encouraged Indians to return to their traditional way of life and to reject the ways of the white settlers; his influence was greatly responsible for the resistance of the Indians to white settlement of the region in the late 1800s

Tom Sneva (1948-   ), born in Spokane; professional race-car driver; won the 1983 Indianapolis 500; became the first driver to break the 200-mile-per-hour barrier, at the 1977 Indy time trials

Isaac Ingalls Stevens (1818-1862), government official; first territorial governor of Washington; surveyed lands later used by the Northern Pacific Railroad

William Francis Thompson (1888-1965), conservationist; directed the fisheries institute at the University of Washington; president of the American Institute of Fishery Research Biologists and other groups concerned with fish preservation

George Vancouver (1758-1798), British explorer; sailed around present-day Vancouver Island; surveyed the Pacific Coast north of San Francisco; wrote *A Voyage of Discovery to the North Pacific Ocean and Around the World in the Years 1790-1795*

JIMMY RODGERS

THEODORE ROETHKE

SEATHL

TOM SNEVA

JONATHAN WAINWRIGHT

GIG YOUNG

Jonathan Mayhew Wainwright (1883-1953), born in Walla Walla; military officer; during World War II, led the defense of Bataan and Corregidor until forced to surrender; later commanded the U.S. Army's Eastern Division; wrote *General Wainwright's Story*

Adam West (1928-   ), born William West Anderson in Walla Walla; actor; best known for his portrayal of the title role in the 1960s television series "Batman"

Marcus Whitman (1802-1847), pioneer, missionary; with his wife, Narcissa, built the Waiilatpu Indian mission near present-day Walla Walla and several other Indian missions in the Oregon Country; was killed by Cayuse Indians who blamed the settlers for a measles epidemic

Narcissa Prentiss Whitman (1808-1847), pioneer, missionary; one of the first two white women to complete the overland journey across the American continent; with her husband, helped establish missions among the Cayuse, Walla Walla, and Umatilla Indians; was killed by Cayuse Indians

Rufus Woods (1878-1954), editor, publisher; published *Wenatchee Daily World* (1907-50); campaigned for the building of Grand Coulee Dam

Audrey May Wurdemann (1911-1960), born in Seattle; poet; won the 1935 Pulitzer Prize in poetry for *Bright Ambush*

Gig Young (1913-1978), actor; lived in Washington; won the 1969 Academy Award for best supporting actor for his role in *They Shoot Horses, Don't They?*; appeared in the television series "The Rogues"

GOVERNORS

Elisha P. Ferry	1889-1893	Albert D. Rossellini	1957-1965
John Harte McGraw	1893-1897	Daniel J. Evans	1965-1977
John Rankin Rogers	1897-1901	Dixy Lee Ray	1977-1981
Henry McBride	1901-1905	John D. Spellman	1981-1985
Albert Edward Mead	1905-1909	Booth Gardner	1985-
Samuel G. Cosgrove	1909		
Marion E. Hay	1909-1913		
Ernest Lister	1913-1919		
Louis Folwell Hart	1919-1925		
Roland H. Hartley	1925-1933		
Clarence D. Martin	1933-1941		
Arthur B. Langlie	1941-1945		
Monrad C. Wallgren	1945-1949		
Arthur B. Langlie	1949-1957		

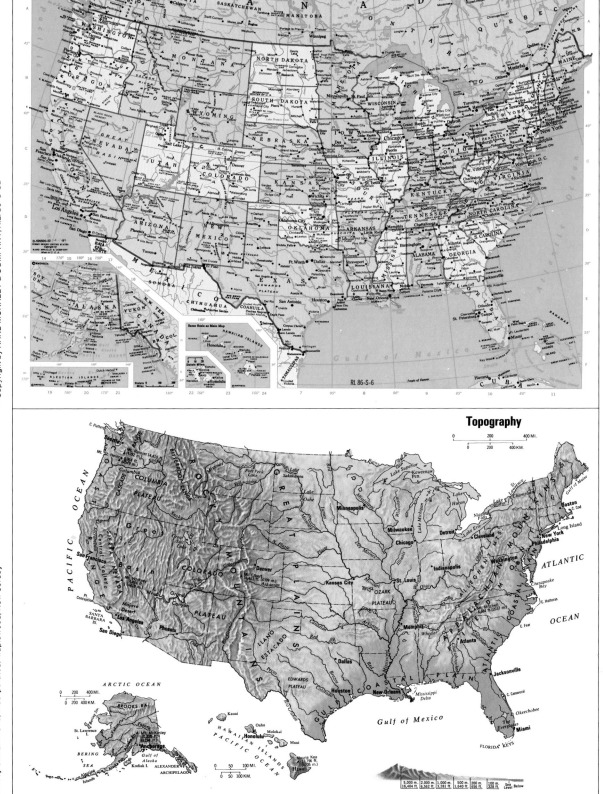

Topography

0   200   400 MI.

0   200   400 KM.

5,000 m.   2,000 m.   1,000 m.   500 m.   200 m.   100 m.   Sea
16,404 ft. 6,562 ft. 3,281 ft. 1,640 ft. 656 ft. 328 ft. Level
                                                              Below

WASHINGTON

BRITISH COLUMBIA

CANADA
U.S.

IDAHO

OREGON

VANCOUVER ISLAND

OLYMPIC NATIONAL PARK

CASCADE RANGE

Seattle
Tacoma
Olympia
Spokane
Yakima
Walla Walla
Bellingham
Everett
Bremerton
Victoria
Esquimalt
Portland
Vancouver
Coeur d'Alene
Moscow
Pullman
Lewiston
Clarkston
Kennewick
Richland
Wenatchee
Ellensburg
Moses Lake
Ephrata
Coulee Dam
Grand Coulee

Pacific Ocean

Strait of Juan de Fuca

Columbia River

Longitude West of Greenwich

A-500648-71

COSMO SERIES WASHINGTON
RAND McNALLY AND COMPANY
Made in U.S.A.

Spokane (inset)

Seattle–Tacoma (inset)

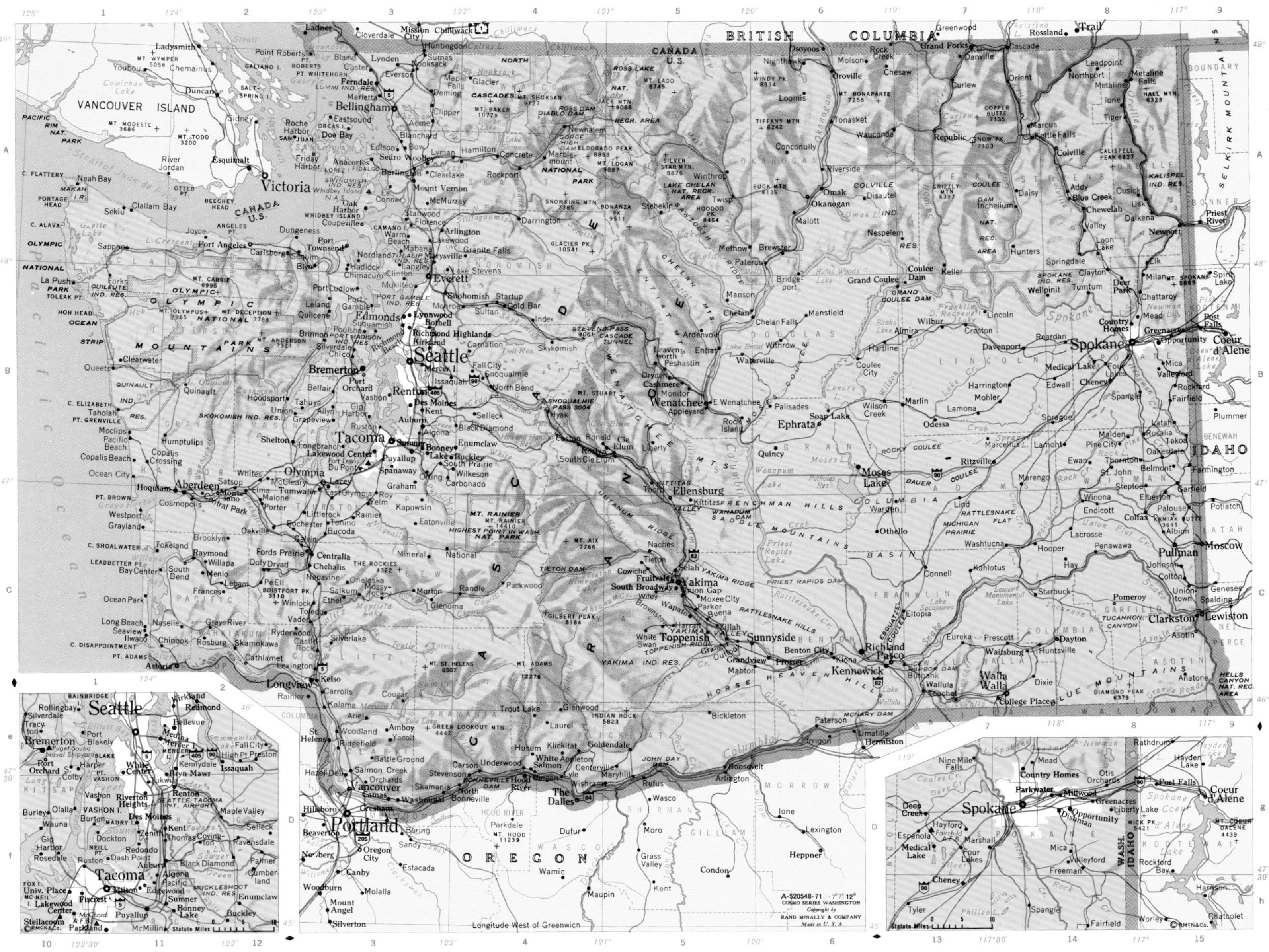

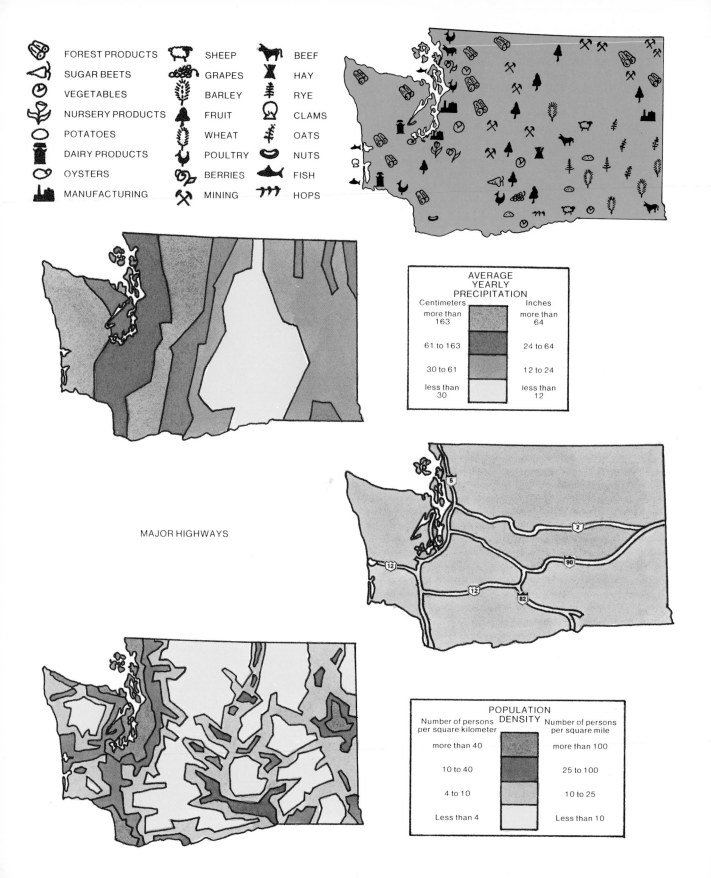

FOREST PRODUCTS   SHEEP   BEEF
SUGAR BEETS   GRAPES   HAY
VEGETABLES   BARLEY   RYE
NURSERY PRODUCTS   FRUIT   CLAMS
POTATOES   WHEAT   OATS
DAIRY PRODUCTS   POULTRY   NUTS
OYSTERS   BERRIES   FISH
MANUFACTURING   MINING   HOPS

AVERAGE
YEARLY
PRECIPITATION

Centimeters   Inches

more than
163   more than
64

61 to 163   24 to 64

30 to 61   12 to 24

less than
30   less than
12

MAJOR HIGHWAYS

POPULATION
Number of persons DENSITY Number of persons
per square kilometer   per square mile

more than 40   more than 100

10 to 40   25 to 100

4 to 10   10 to 25

Less than 4   Less than 10

TOPOGRAPHY

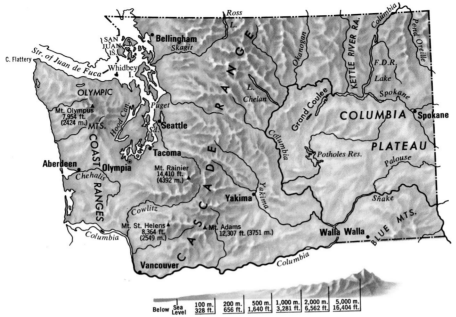

Courtesy of Hammond, Incorporated
Maplewood, New Jersey

COUNTIES

The waterfront in La Conner

INDEX

Page numbers that appear in boldface type indicate illustrations

**The Dungeness
River in the
Olympic Mountains**

Picture Identifications
Front cover: Mount Rainier and Edith Creek
Pages 2-3: Cape Disappointment Lighthouse
Page 6: Old-growth Douglas fir trees in Mount Rainier National Park
Pages 8-9: The southeast side of Mount Rainier
Pages 20-21: Montage of Washington residents
Pages 26-27: *Indian Camp Colville*, a painting by Paul Kane depicting a Nez Perce village
Pages 38-39: A painting by P.A. Morgan of the Seattle waterfront in the 1800s
Pages 51-52: Wheat fields in southeastern Washington
Page 68: The state capitol in Olympia
Pages 78-79: Fox Harbor on Sucia Island in the San Juan Islands
Pages 88-89: The Seattle skyline
Page 108: Montage of state symbols, including the state flag, state tree (western hemlock), state bird (willow goldfinch), state flower (coast rhododendron), and state gem (petrified wood)
Back cover: Seattle's Space Needle at night

Picture Acknowledgments

Front cover, 2-3, 4, © **Steve Terrill;** 5, © **Robert Frerck/Odyssey Productions;** 6, 8-9, 11, 12, 13, 14 (two photos), 15, © **John Marshall;** 16, © **Reidar Hahn;** 17 (two photos), © **Steve Terrill;** 19, 20 (top left), © **John Marshall;** 20 (top right), © **Virginia Grimes;** 20 (bottom left), © **Lee Balterman/Marilyn Gartman Agency;** 20 (bottom right), © **Kirkendall/Spring;** 21 (top left, top right, bottom left), © **John Marshall;** 21 (bottom right), © **Kirkendall/Spring;** 23, © **John Marshall;** 26-27, **Courtesy of the Royal Ontario Museum, Toronto, Canada;** 29 (left), © **Steve Terrill;** 29 (right), © **Harvey S. Rice;** 30, **Museum of History and Industry, Seattle WA;** 34 (left), **Oregon Historical Society;** 34 (right), © **John Marshall;** 37 (left), © **Joan Dunlop;** 37 (right), **Oregon Historical Society;** 38-39, **Museum of History and Industry, Seattle, WA;** 41, **North Wind;** 44, 45, **Museum of History and Industry, Seattle, WA;** 46, 47 (two photos), 49, **Washington State Historical Society;** 50, **Museum of History and Industry, Seattle, WA;** 52-53, © **John Marshall;** 55 (left), **Washington State Historical Society;** 55 (right), © **John Marshall;** 56, **Washington State Historical Society;** 59, **Museum of History and Industry, Seattle, WA;** 60 (two photos), **Washington State Historical Society;** 63, **AP/Wide World Photos;** 65 (two photos), © **Ed Cooper/H. Armstrong Roberts;** 66 (left), © **John Marshall;** 66 (right), © **R. Lamb/H. Armstrong Roberts;** 67 (left), © **John Marshall;** 67 (right), © **Steve Terrill;** 68, © **Kirkendall/Spring;** 71 (left), © **John Marshall;** 71 (right), © **Steve Terrill;** 72 (left), © **John Marshall;** 72 (right), © **Kirkendall/Spring;** 73 (two photos), 74 (left), © **John Marshall;** 74 (right), **Root Resources;** 75, **Cameramann International, Ltd.;** 76, © **Steve Terrill;** 78-79, © **John Marshall;** 81 (left), **Courtesy of the Museum of Native American Cultures;** 81 (right), © **Al Guiteras/Journalism Services;** 82 (left), **Seattle Art Museum;** 82 (right), © **Roger Schreiber;** 85 (left), © **Bob & Ira Spring;** 85 (right), 87, 88-89, 91, 93, © **John Marshall;** 93 (map), **Len Meents;** 95, © **Steve Terrill;** 96, © **W. D. McKinney/SuperStock:** 97, © **Ed Cooper/H. Armstrong Roberts;** 98 (left), © **Chad Slattery/Tony Stone Worldwide;** 98 (right), © **M. Loken/H. Armstrong Roberts;** 98 (map), **Len Meents;** 99, © **Lee Foster;** 100 (left), © **Ruth A. Smith/Root Resources;** 100 (right), © **Biedel/Photri;** 102 (left), © **Steve Terrill;** 102 (right), 103, © **Bob & Ira Spring;** 103 (map), **Len Meents;** 104 (two photos), © **John Marshall;** 106, © **Wally Hampton/Marilyn Gartman Agency;** 106 (map), **Len Meents;** 107, © **John Marshall;** 108 (tree), © **Greg Vaughn/Tom Stack & Associates;** 108 (flag), **Courtesy Flag Research Center, Winchester, Massachusetts 01890;** 108 (bird), © **J. Robert Woodward/Cornell Laboratory of Ornithology;** 108 (flowers), © **Tom Coker/SuperStock;** 108 (petrified wood), © **Bob & Ira Spring;** 111, © **James Blank/Root Resources;** 112, © **Steve Terrill;** 113, © **Joura/H. Armstrong Roberts;** 115, © **Steve Terrill;** 116 (two photos), © **John Marshall;** 120, © **Kirkendall/Spring;** 125, © **John Marshall;** 126, 127 (Brown, Channing, Crosby), **AP/Wide World Photos;** 127 (Ballinger), **North Wind;** 128 (four photos), 129 (Hendrix, Joffrey, Livingstone), **AP/Wide World Photos;** 129 (Hill), **North Wind;** 130 (four photos), 131 (Roethke, Rodgers, Sneva), **AP/Wide World Photos;** 131 (Seathl), **Historical Pictures Service, Chicago;** 132 (two photos), **AP/Wide World Photos;** 136, **Len Meents;** 138, © **Steve Terrill;** 141, © **John Marshall;** back cover, © Alan Bolestra/**Third Coast Stock Source**

About the Author

R. Conrad Stein was born and grew up in Chicago. He always aspired to be a writer and began writing professionally shortly after his graduation from the University of Illinois. He is the author of many books and short stories for young readers.

To prepare for this book, Mr. Stein traveled in the cities and countryside of Washington and chatted with the people. He was overwhelmed by Washington's great beauty and the friendliness of its residents. Mr. Stein lives in Chicago with his wife and their daughter Janna.